PLAYING AND TEACHING THE STRINGS

Series editor: Charles R. Hoffer
Indiana University

Brass Ensemble Method for Music Educators
Jay D. Zorn, University of Southern California

Percussion Manual
F. Michael Combs, The University of Tennessee, Knoxville

Playing and Teaching the Strings
Vincent Oddo, Northeastern Illinois University

PLAYING AND TEACHING THE STRINGS

Vincent Oddo
Northeastern Illinois University

WADSWORTH PUBLISHING COMPANY
BELMONT, CALIFORNIA
A Division of Wadsworth, Inc.

For Bonnie, Julie, and Danny

Music Editor: Sheryl Fullerton

Editorial/production services by
Phoenix Publishing Services, San Francisco

Printed in the United States of America

1 2 3 4 5 6 7 8 9 10—83 82 81 80 79

Library of Congress Cataloging in Publication Data

Oddo, Vincent.
    Playing and teaching the strings.

    Includes bibliography and index.
    1.   Stringed instruments, Bowed—Instruction and study.   I.   Title.
MT259.03   787'.01'071   79-12950
ISBN 0-534-00614-0

CONTENTS

MUSICAL EXCERPTS

EDITOR'S FOREWORD

Instruction in instruments is an important part of the training of future instrumental music teachers. Part of their future success as teachers depends on their knowledge of instruments other than their major instrument. Learning "minor" or "secondary" instruments has two parts. One is a basic ability in playing the instrument—fingerings, embouchure, playing position, and so on. The other part is a knowledge of how to teach the instrument to students at the beginning and intermediate levels. These two aspects of instruction in instruments are by no means contradictory. However, sometimes students in such classes or lessons concentrate almost exclusively on learning to play the instrument, which leaves them deficient in teaching knowledge. In other cases, such instruction contains little playing of music, and therefore the learning that results is largely a "head" knowledge based on limited practical understanding.

The WADSWORTH SERIES IN CLASS INSTRUMENTAL METHODS seeks to bring together the best of both the playing and teaching sides of the secondary instrument instruction. These books contain material for the future instrumental teachers to learn to play. There is also information about how to teach the instrument to beginning students.

The WADSWORTH SERIES books are basically ensemble methods books. Since there is seldom time in undergraduate music education curriculums for instruction on individual instruments, like instruments are learned at the same time in the same class. Because of the variety of instruments available, more interesting music can be performed.

Playing and Teaching the Strings by Vincent Oddo of Northeastern Illinois University was selected for inclusion in the WADSWORTH SERIES IN CLASS INSTRUMENTAL METHODS because it contains the features of information about teaching as well as material to play. Also, it includes all relevant string instruments. Of equal importance, however, is the fact that it is a tested class-string methods textbook that is based on years of experience in teaching such classes. It is specifically designed with the future instrumental-music teacher in mind. In short, it is well suited to meet the needs of a secondary string-class textbook.

Charles R. Hoffer
Indiana University

PREFACE

The training of a string teacher is largely dependent upon instructional materials that combine both musical and practical information. In addition, the future string teacher must have organized information and experiences in both playing *and* teaching the instruments.

Strings provides future instrumental music teachers, whether string players or not, with a balanced presentation of:

1. Basic instruction in playing the violin, viola, cello, and string bass; holding the instruments correctly; basic left- and right-hand techniques; tuning, care, and maintenance of the instruments and bows, etc.; and

2. Suggestions, materials, and teaching strategies for creating and sustaining an effective string program in the schools.

Of these two aspects, the second has too often been treated superficially, with the acquisition of important practical information left generally to chance.

Strings differs from other class instrumental methods texts in that it presents an extensive and balanced presentation of information on *both* the musical and practical aspects of string instruction. In doing so, it brings together under one cover a variety of material—material available only through laborious and time-consuming research into a number of sources.

In addition to the instructional materials on how to play and teach the instruments, here are just a few of the unique features contained in *Strings*:

The physics affecting sound production and tone control

Bowing and fingering conventions

Exercises for editing bowings and fingerings

Making minor repairs and adjustments

Evaluating and selecting instruments, music, equipment, and accessories

Along with these, the book also has a comprehensive Appendix containing graded materials, source materials, bibliography, films, and other supplementary information.

An important feature of *Strings* is its ensemble approach. This format affords students in the string methods classes the opportunity to observe the different types of problems associated with individual instruments, to perform a variety of representative string chamber music, and to explore those musical aspects that contribute to basic musicianship: intonation, phrasing, balance, articulation, and other performance concepts.

The seven chapters follow a logical progression, one that closely approximates the learning/teaching sequence encountered in a classroom setting. Chapters 1 and 2 emphasize the formulation of basic left- and right-hand techniques. Chapters 3 and 4 build on this foundation and introduce intermediate techniques. Chapter 3 was specifically designed to provide materials that the students could use to develop added facility on their own, thus saving valuable classtime. Chapters 5 and 6 further solidify the techniques of previous chapters while introducing additional concepts. Throughout all chapters there are liberal suggestions for teaching these concepts and techniques. The remaining chapter presents a thorough overview of "on-the-job" types of information.

Finally, the author is aware that no one volume can adequately contain a complete study of even one instrument, let alone be definitive when both the musical and practical aspects of teaching the strings are combined. The main purpose of *Strings* was to set forth in a systematic and balanced approach those materials that will provide the knowledge that is essential to the success of the prospective string teacher.

ACKNOWLEDGMENTS

I wish to express my thanks to the music students at Northeastern Illinois University and the following reviewers for their many helpful comments: Marcia Ferritto, Wittenberg University; Steven Heyde, West Virginia University; Kelly Martino, North Texas State University; and Sharon McCreery, Cottey College.

For their technical assistance I wish to thank Terry Alexander for her editorial contributions; Mike Foley and Rich Sato of the Northeastern Photo Lab for their fine illustrations; and Hinda Keller Farber who copyedited the final manuscript.

A special gratitude is extended to some of my former teachers, colleagues and friends who contributed indirectly to the completion of this book: Samuel Arron, Charles Schell, Patrick Gardner, Leon Stein, and William Primrose.

Finally, I am especially indebted to Charles Hoffer of Indiana University for his advice, encouragement, and many valued contributions.

Vincent Oddo

TO THE STUDENT

More than any other family of instruments, the strings possess an almost unlimited vocabulary of expressive effects. From the unaccompanied instrument to the symphony orchestra, the sound of the strings is generally accepted as one of the most beautiful in music. Their dynamic range and richness of color are almost unequaled, and their emotional power can never be underestimated. Their enormous breadth of musical expressiveness stretches from the exotic to the sublime, from the transparent to the majestic.

These qualities have made the strings, in a variety of combinations, an attractive medium for the great composers. While strings form the backbone of chamber and symphonic music, their unique timbres also make them compatible with keyboard, wind, brass, and percussion instruments—individually or in ensembles. Their capacity for agility, coupled with the loveliness of an indefinitely sustainable sonority, appeals to a variety of emotions.

Recognizing that these qualities exist as the means of expression for the string musician, their preservation can be sustained solely through the continual development of young musicians whose knowledge, attitudes, and playing abilities are equal to the highest levels of string playing in America. The contribution you can make to help realize this goal is largely dependent upon your ability to: (1) cultivate and maintain interest in strings, (2) demonstrate and teach the essentials of string playing, (3) develop in your students attitudes toward and an awareness of the unique characteristics of string music, and (4) administer your string program. The materials presented here follow a sequence leading to the attainment of these abilities.

Chapter 1

FIRST APPROACHES TO PLAYING AND TEACHING THE STRINGS

PARTS OF THE INSTRUMENTS AND BOWS

Instruments

Figure 1-2 (p. 2) illustrates and identifies the parts that are common to all string instruments—with the obvious exceptions of the chin rest for the violin and viola, the end-pin for the cello and string bass, and the mechanical tuning mechanism for the string bass.

There are many similarities between the four members of the string family, but when the instruments are compared side by side, their differences become very apparent. Before we begin to make these comparisons and note differences, we will have to master the language used to describe the parts of the instruments. Knowing the correct term to use when describing the parts of the instruments (as well as the bow) can be very helpful in other ways. In teaching some-one else to play any instrument, it is important to be able to refer correctly to certain parts. For example, terminology is necessary when illustrating or correcting the position of the thumb on the *neck*, finger position on the *fingerboard*, bow distance from the *bridge*, and so forth. Also, use of the correct term is essential when directing a repair-man to a specific problem if any repairs or adjustments are necessary.

Violin/viola. The soprano (violin) and alto (viola) members of the string family are illustrated in Figure 1-1. (The differences between bows are discussed in the next section of this chapter.) Since most of the dimensions of the violin and viola are direct expansions and contractions of an ideal pattern established by the early seventeenth-century Italian instrument makers, a casual observer can not immediately see the differences between the two unless the instruments are compared directly.

In comparing the instruments, it is obvious that the viola is slightly larger than the violin in all its dimensions. The subtler visual differences lie in the width of the ribs, width of the lower bout, and sometimes the shape of the pegbox where it joins the neck, just below the fingerboard nut.

Cello/bass. The tenor (cello) and bass members of the string family are illustrated in Figure 1-3. Here the differences in the dimensions are very real: The string bass is almost twice the size of the cello. But closer observation will reveal some other visual differences. The shoulders of the upper bouts of the cello are rounded; on the bass they slope. The cello—like the violin and viola— has its strings tuned with pegs and string tuners; on the bass this is done with a mechanical tuning mechanism (see Figure 1-4). A profile view of the bass and cello may sometimes show a difference in the amount of curvature in the backs of the instruments.

Bows

The bows, like the instruments, evolved through several stages over a period of centuries before reaching their present form. The parts that are common to all bows are illustrated in Figure 1-5. For the bow as for the instruments, it is important to memorize the names of the various parts.

Violin   Viola

Figure 1-1

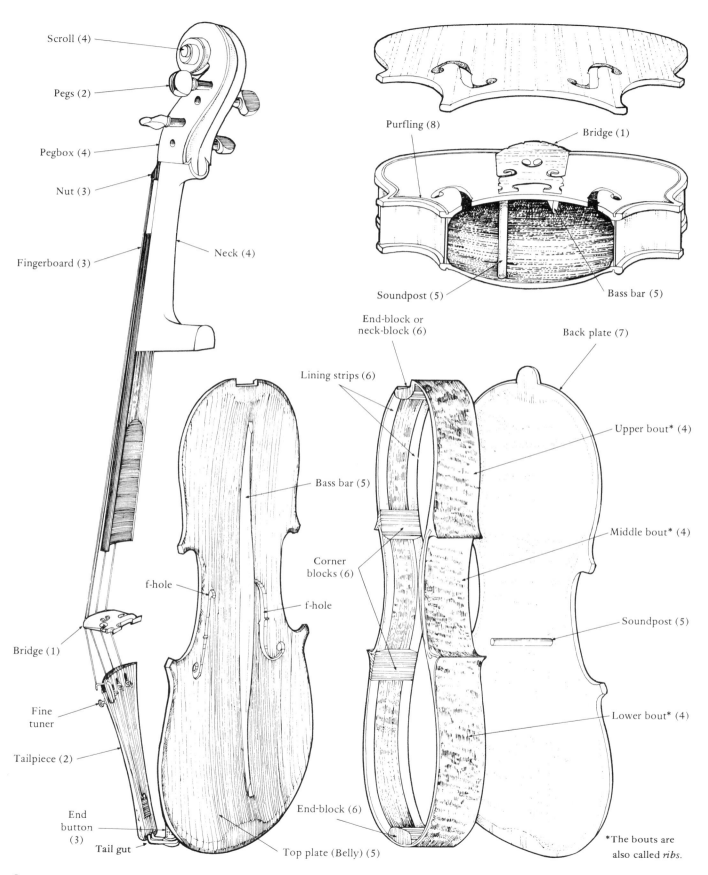

Scroll (4)

Pegs (2)

Pegbox (4)

Nut (3)

Fingerboard (3)

Neck (4)

Purfling (8)

Bridge (1)

Soundpost (5)

Bass bar (5)

End-block or neck-block (6)

Back plate (7)

Lining strips (6)

Bass bar (5)

Upper bout* (4)

Corner blocks (6)

Middle bout* (4)

Soundpost (5)

f-hole

f-hole

Bridge (1)

Fine tuner

Tailpiece (2)

Lower bout* (4)

End button (3)

Tail gut

End-block (6)

Top plate (Belly) (5)

*The bouts are also called *ribs*.

String Bass   Cello

Figure 1–3

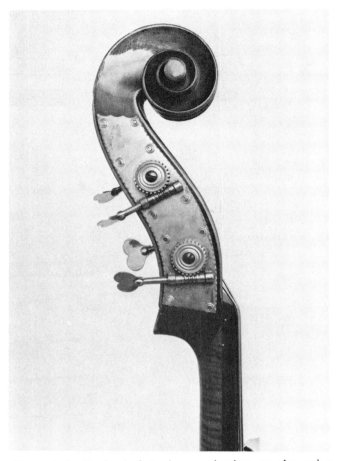

Figure 1–4. Mechanical tuning mechanism on the string bass.

Comparison of bows. Figure 1–6 illustrates the five bows commonly used with the instruments of the string family. Except for weight and the slightly thicker stick and frog, there is very little difference between the viola and violin bows. Viola bows are a bit longer than violin bows, but only by about 3/16 of an inch. The stick and frog of the cello bows are proportionately thicker than violin and viola bows. However, the stick of the cello bow is shorter and has the characteristic "swan-shaped" head. The French bass bow is only 1/16 of an inch shorter than the cello bow, but the diameter of the stick, size of the frog, and weight are almost twice that of the cello bow. The German or But-

Figure 1–2. The parts common to all string instruments. The materials used are (1) Hard maple; (2) Ebony, rosewood, or boxwood; (3) Ebony; (4) Curly maple; (5) Spruce; (6) Spruce or willow; (7) Curly maple (sometimes pear or sycamore); (8) Layers of one strip of white poplar between two layers of black-dyed pearwood. From Carleen Maley Hutchins, "The Physics of Violins." Copyright © 1962 by Scientific American, Inc. All rights reserved.

ler bow is distinctive in the width of the frog and the length of the bow screw button.

Bow hair. Bows are strung with about 120 to 150 strands of horsehair. The best quality bow hair comes from Siberian or Northwest Canadian prairie horses. The quality of bow hair is judged by its ability to grip the string while producing a smooth, unbroken sound. How it wears, or the time between rehairings, is another factor to consider when measuring quality. Horsehair is very costly, and the search for a suitable substitute has not been very successful. Some synthetic hair is currently available, but the quality is adequate for student bows only.

Bow hair surface. In some current references to bow hair, there still exists the *false* notion that the surface is covered with little teeth, somewhat akin to a saw blade. The photographs in Figure 1–7, however, reveal a surface that bears little resemblance to the saw-tooth conception. These photographs were taken through a scanning electron microscope and provide the evidence and detail not possible by other means.

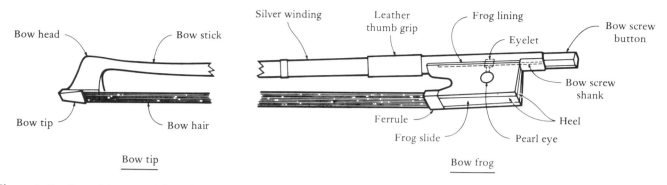

Bow tip

Bow frog

Figure 1–5. Copyright material used through permission of Niel A. Kjos Music Company, Park Ridge, Illinois.

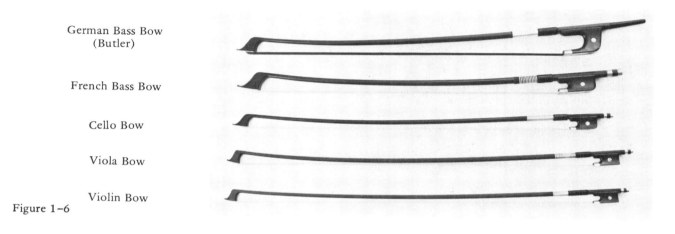

German Bass Bow
(Butler)

French Bass Bow

Cello Bow

Viola Bow

Violin Bow

Figure 1–6

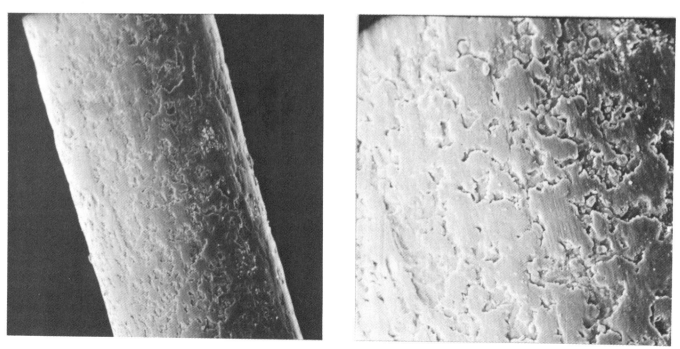

Figure 1–7. Bow hair surface, magnified 250 times (left) and 650 times (right).
Photographs courtesy of G. T. Chubb, Argonne National Laboratory.

Rosin. A fresh, clean bow hair will not produce a very audible sound until it has been rosined. When rosin is applied, its brittle and sticky particles cling to the surface of the hair and cause the strings to vibrate through abrasive action.*

HOLDING THE INSTRUMENTS AND BOWS

Steps to Holding the Instruments

The proper playing position is the first and perhaps most important aspect of beginning string teaching. It is the base upon which all subsequent techniques must rest. Since students will have to learn two distinctly different tasks (holding the instrument and holding the bow), each task should be introduced separately.

There is always the question of whether to begin a class with the violins and violas in the *standing* or *sitting* position.** Both approaches can be successful, and each offers several distinct advantages. In the sitting position: (1) the students are more comfortable, more relaxed; (2) they receive essential preparation for ensemble playing; (3) visibility is increased—the line of sight between the instructor and the student is not blocked by other students; (4) the chance of accidental damage to the instrument or bow is minimized. For the standing position (violins and violas): (1) at the introductory level, the mechanics of movement are more easily integrated because of the motion of the body as a whole; (2) muscular tension tends to be lessened; (3) the students gain an earlier awareness of the interrelationship between arms, body, and balance.

At this point consideration must be given to the type of chair used, because the wrong kind can interfere with the establishment of the correct playing position. Generally, the design of the chair should be the nonsloping (flat seat) type with a straight back. The standard sized chair, while not ideal, can be adequate for the small violinist or violist, but is totally unsatisfactory for the small cellist. Since the knees of the cellist play a direct role in the support and positioning of the instrument, the height of the chair is critical and must be sized to the student. The height of the chair should permit the cellist's feet to rest flat on the floor forming a 90 degree angle between the upper and lower leg. A variety of different chair sizes should be kept on hand for this reason.

Some Preliminary Procedures

Instrument identification. Prior to issue, all instruments, cases, and covers should be numbered and labeled with complete student and content identification. For cello and

---

*How and when to apply rosin are discussed on page 23.

**The sitting position for the string bass player should not be introduced until the student has had considerable playing experience in the *standing* position, and only if a stool of correct size (30 inches) or an adjustable bass chair is available.

string basses, a baggage-type tag may be tied to the strap handles of the canvas covers.

Correct size instruments. In the school string program, selecting the correct size instrument and bow for *each* student can spell the difference between success and failure. Suggestions for measuring the students and for selecting the correct size and number of different instruments to keep on hand are contained in Chapter 7.

Complete outfit. Whether school, rental, or student-owned instruments, each must be a complete outfit of bow, case, rosin, shoulder pads for violins and violas, and end-pin holders for cellos and string basses. All bow clamps, case locks, snaps and zippers, straps and handles must be secure and checked frequently. In addition, the equipment must be in perfect adjustment.

Shoulder pads. To achieve the proper position and encourage a relaxed and natural posture, the use of a shoulder pad is strongly recommended for the violins and violas. Because of the individual physical difference between students, the thickness of the pad will vary. The shoulder pad is a proper fit when the student can support the instrument without raising the left shoulder or pressing the jaw excessively into the chin rest. The composition of the pad may be any soft material—foam or sponge rubber, a cloth-filled bag, etc. The pad should be rectangular in shape and cover an area about twice the size of the chin rest. Fasten the shoulder pad on the back side of the instrument—opposite the chin rest—with a rubber band stretched from the lower corner block to the end button (see Figure 1–8).

Working plan. As you begin to teach how to hold the instruments and bows, you must establish an efficient working pattern. The following points should be included in whatever plan proves to be the most efficient:

1. Open the cases and handle the instruments away from obstructions. One possibility is to place the cases and instruments a few feet in front of the students. This will allow them to observe how the instrument or bow should be handled when removed from the case.

2. Work with one student at a time, while encouraging the rest of the class to act as observers.

3. Demonstrate and explain all aspects of holding and playing the instruments *before* directly instructing individual students.

4. Be systematic. Teach one instrument at a time and create a routine that is a predictable pattern so students know clearly what to expect.

5. For added reinforcement, repeat all demonstrations several times.

6. Verify the quality of your instruction by asking your students to teach you.

7. Keep the physical aspects of playing the instruments separate from music making. Introduce all

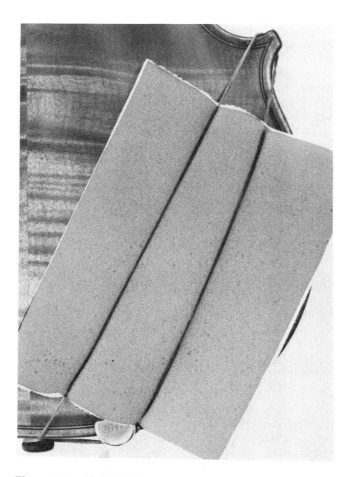

Figure 1–8. Violin/viola shoulder pad.

Figure 1–9. Violin or viola: playing position.

new techniques through the *rote approach*. This will permit students to focus their concentration on the technique—not the interpretation of a music symbol.

8. In early instruction, physically assist students in achieving the techniques being studied: set their hands on the instruments, help them draw the bow, etc.

9. Once students have achieved a satisfactory position of some physical "set," ask them to memorize that sensation.

Common errors. As your class progresses, the responsibility for holding and playing the instrument naturally shifts to the student. As this happens, there will be occasions when one or more of the conditions to achieve—cited in the following sections—will slip out of "set." To a very large extent, the art of teaching the strings requires cataloguing *visual reference points.* Any deviation from the ideal "picture" of correct posture and application of techniques is readily observable once these visual reference points are memorized. They are both the indicator and the solution to the problem. The figures and commentary that follow will help to illustrate and direct your attention to these refer-

ence points; also, a listing of common errors of holding and playing the instruments—and holding and playing with the bow—is given at the end of the sections related to each of the instruments. Review these and the figures periodically; they are the fundamentals for successfully diagnosing and correcting errors.

Sitting Position

Violin and viola. Show that the violinist and violist will sit somewhat forward on the chair, back erect, with both feet flat on the floor. The right foot is usually slightly behind the left foot. The feet, however, should not be "locked" over specific spots. Students should feel free to adjust this position slightly to prevent tension. Figure 1–9 shows an acceptable sitting position, with the instrument in the playing position.

Cello. The cellist sits well-forward on the chair; the back is straight, with the body leaning slightly forward. Both feet are flat on the floor, and are generally located opposite each other. Because the positioning of the feet will affect the position of the cello, no exact placement can or should be given. More will be said about this problem when we discuss how to hold the instrument. Figure 1–10 shows an acceptable sitting posture, with the cello in the playing position.

Preparatory and Playing Positions

In this chapter we will discuss two types of positions: preparatory and playing. The latter will be refined further in the next chapter, when finger placement and patterns are introduced.

Preparatory position. This position is used mainly to help the student gain confidence in holding or supporting the instrument and to introduce basic concepts of the left-hand and -arm positions.

Playing position. This position, being an extension of the preparatory position, is used to refine the attitude, posture, or "set" of the left-hand and -arm position. It will also serve as the position for introducing finger placement.

Only after the students have achieved the conditions outlined for the preparatory position should they advance

to the playing position. However, either position may be used for open string studies—for plucking the strings (pizzicato) with the right hand or playing with the bow (arco).

Holding the Violin and Viola

Preparatory position. Working with one student at a time, remove the instrument from the case, attach the shoulder pad, and set it under the student's right arm—between the elbow and body. Refer to this as "rest position 1" (see Figure 1–11). This position is used for extended rest periods. A second type of rest position is illustrated in Figure 1–12. This position is used for relatively shorter periods of rest.

With the instrument in the position illustrated in Figure 1–11, set the student's left hand on the upper bout so that the large knuckles are centered over the upper rib, the ball of the thumb rests on the center of the back of the instrument, and the fingers rest on the top of the instrument. From this position, show the student how to raise the instrument and set it on his left shoulder (see Figure 1–13). The instrument is pulled toward the neck with the left arm so that the end button is a little to the left of the "Adam's apple." While keeping the head erect, the student should

Figure 1–10. Cello: playing position.

Figure 1–11. Rest position 1.

Figure 1–12. Rest position 2.

Figure 1–13. Preparatory position.

turn his head slightly to the left (between 1/8 and 1/16 turn) and set the *jaw* into the chin rest. The chin rest should contact the jaw midway between the center of the chin and the left ear. When properly positioned, the instrument will be tilted slightly to the right and at approximately a 35° angle from the shoulders. This position will serve as the introductory position for open string exercises.

Refer to Figures 1–14 through 1–16 as you read the following points:

1. Both shoulders should be in a normal, relaxed position. *Error:* Left shoulder is raised to meet the shoulder pad. If the student cannot keep the shoulder relaxed while supporting the instrument, the fit of the shoulder pad may be incorrect.

2. When the student places the side of the jaw on the chin rest, the head must remain erect. *Error:* The head falls to the left or right and excessive pressure is applied with the jaw to the chin rest, or the tip of the chin and not the jaw is placed on the chin rest (see Figures 1–15 and 1–16). Reposition the instrument and recheck the fitting of the shoulder pad.

3. Left elbow must be away from the body and under the center of the instrument, keeping the fingerboard parallel to the floor. Violists, however, may

carry the scroll somewhat lower than violinists. Length and weight are the factors here. *Error:* Elbow is too far to the player's left or rests against the body, allowing the instrument to sag toward the floor.

4. Left wrist should be bent slightly toward the scroll. *Error:* The wrist is collapsed with the palm of the hand under the back of the instrument.

5. While keeping the fingerboard parallel to the floor, the top of the instrument should be tilted slightly to the player's right. *Error:* There is no tilt, or the player swings the instrument toward the center of the body. This may be caused by a poorly fitting shoulder pad, improper placement of the jaw on the chin rest, or wrong positioning of the end button in relation to the neck.

Playing position. With the instrument held securely between the jaw and shoulder, show your students how to slide the left hand from the upper bout back to the end of the fingerboard. During this position change, the points cited for the establishment of the preparatory position must be preserved.

To insure the proper "set" of the left hand, assist your students in achieving the following conditions. As you do this, refer to Figures 1–17 through 1–21.

1. The pad of the thumb is held lightly against the side of the neck on a spot slightly below the juncture of the fingerboard and neck, and at approximately one inch forward of the nut at the end of the fingerboard. The thumb should be straight or bent slightly so that the tip of the thumb is curved *away* from the

Figure 1–14. Compare the positions of the head, shoulders, and arm between the correct version illustrated here, and the incorrect postures of Figures 1–15 and 1–16.

Figure 1–15. Incorrect preparatory position.

Figure 1–16. Incorrect preparatory position.

fingerboard. Again, because of individual physical differences, the amount of thumb projecting above or below this spot will vary from student to student. Students with rather short fingers will feel more comfortable placing the pad of the thumb on a spot somewhat lower than the above recommendation. The reverse placement of the thumb (higher) will be satisfactory for students with longer fingers. The inside of the index finger, just above the large knuckle, is placed lightly against the other side of the fingerboard. Its location is somewhat behind the thumb. All fingers should be rounded over the strings. This position will serve to introduce finger placement on the strings (Chapter 2).

2. The left wrist should be bent only slightly toward the scroll, while the sides of the wrist are kept perfectly straight, in line with the sides of the forearm.

3. In the early stages of instruction, the elbow must always be under the center of the instrument. Later, its position will vary depending upon which string is being played.

4. The forearm should be rotated to bring the heel of the palm almost parallel to the fingerboard.

Common errors

1. Thumb is too far forward of the index finger.
2. Left wrist is bent toward the instrument and not the scroll—Figures 1–19 and 1–20.
3. Fingers are not over the fingerboard with palm heel *away* from fingerboard—Figure 1–21.

4. Elbow is too far to the left or exaggeratedly to the right—Figures 1–15 and 1–16.
5. The neck has fallen into the crotch of the hand.
6. Tip—not pad—of the thumb is on the neck.

Holding the Cello

Preparatory position. Working with one student at a time, slide the bow from its pouch and set it aside. Next, remove

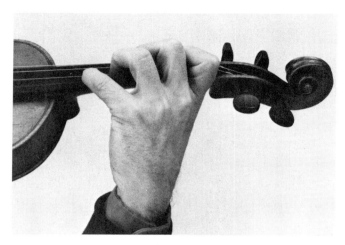

Figure 1–17. Compare the positions of the thumb, fingers, and wrist between the correct illustrations of Figures 1–17 and 1–18, and incorrect versions of Figures 1–19 through 1–21.

Figure 1–18. Correct playing position.

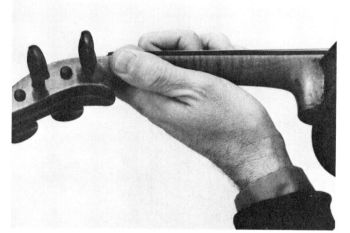

Figure 1–19. Incorrect playing position.

Figure 1–20. Incorrect playing position.

Figure 1–21. Incorrect playing position.

the instrument from its cover. Adjust and lock the end pin to about one foot in length, set it in an end-pin holder, and proceed as follows (see Figure 1–22):

1. With the player sitting erect and forward on the chair, feet flat on the floor, set the cello between the student's knees so that the curve of the lower bout (on the right side) is against the inside of the right knee. The left knee will contact the instrument behind the corner of the left bout.

2. Readjust the end of the end pin so that the rim of the upper bout (right side) rests against the student's chest at a point just below the rib cage.

3. Position the instrument so that the scroll and neck clear the student's shoulder. The neck of the cello should be no more than one or two inches to the

Figure 1-22. Cello: preparatory position.

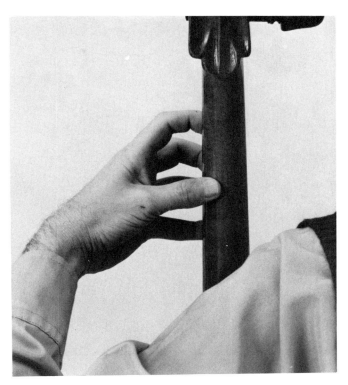

Figure 1-23. Compare the positions of the thumb, fingers, and wrist between the correct illustrations—Figures 1-23 and 1-24—and the incorrect versions—Figures 1-25 and 1-26.

left of the player's head, with the lowest tuning peg opposite the player's left ear.

4. The cello is tilted slightly to the player's right. This will facilitate playing on the highest string when the bow is used.

5. As a reference point, the end pin should be positioned between 12:00 and 1:00 on an imaginary clock face—with 12 o'clock directly in front of the student.

6. Set the player's left thumb in the curve of the neck heel with the fingers over the strings.

7. Position the left elbow at a 45° angle away from the body.

8. The top of the wrist should be positioned so that there is the appearance of a gently curved line from the tip of the elbow to the knuckles.

Playing position. When the students can stabilize the instrument between their knees—without applying pressure—show them how to slide their hands from the preparatory position (thumb on the curve of the neck heel) to the end of the fingerboard. To insure the proper "set" of the left hand, assist your students in the achievement of the following conditions (see Figures 1-23 through 1-26).

Figure 1-24. Correct playing position.

Figure 1–25. Incorrect playing position.

Figure 1–26. Incorrect playing position.

Figure 1–27. Preparatory position.

1. The pad of the thumb rests lightly on the center of the underside of the neck. For a full-sized cello, the thumb is about 3½ inches from the end of the fingerboard. The thumb position will shift slightly to the left of center when the fingers move from higher to lower strings.

2. When the thumb is centered under the neck, the second finger should be directly over it, with the remaining fingers wellrounded over the strings so that the hand forms a letter *C* from the tip of the thumb to the tip of the second finger.

3. The forearm and wrist are in a straight line from the tip of the elbow to the large knuckles. The elbow will be positioned at a 45° angle away from the body.

4. The shoulders are relaxed and parallel to the floor.

Common errors

1. Right knee extends beyond the lower bout—too far forward. This will interfere with the bowing on the lowest string.

2. Placement or length of end pin is incorrect, causing the neck of the instrument to rest on the student's shoulder and the rim of the upper bout to slip below the rib cage.

3. Thumb is under index finger or too far to the right of center.

4. Wrist is collapsed toward the neck.

5. Elbow is too close to the body, causing the wrist to point away from the instrument.

Figure 1-28. Playing position.

6. The angle of tilt of the instrument toward the right is either excessive or insufficient. Both will make for awkward bowing on the outside strings.

Holding the Bass

Preparatory position. Working with one student at a time, slide the bow from the pouch and set it aside. Next, remove the string bass from its cover, adjust and lock the end pin and set it on an end-pin holder,* and proceed as follows (see Figures 1-27 through 1-29):

1. Show the students how to position their feet so that they will be standing in back and to the right of the instrument. The location of the right foot will be approximately 5 inches to the right of the left foot and 7 inches behind it. The right foot should also be approximately 2½ feet behind and at a 45° angle from the end pin.

2. Adjust the length of the end pin so that the lowest tuning key is opposite the player's left ear, and the nut at the end of the fingerboard is level with the student's eyes.

*If the end pin is equipped with a rubber tip, an end-pin holder may not be necessary.

Figure 1-29. Compare the position of the feet, angle of the instrument, and distance of scroll in relationship to the head between the correct illustrations in Figures 1-27 and 1-28, and this incorrect version.

3. The bass is inclined toward the player, with the back of the upper bout resting against the left groin.

4. The left knee is bent and placed against the back of the instrument with the majority of weight on the right leg.

5. The instrument is tilted slightly to the player's right. The amount of tilt depends upon whether the French or German bow is used—generally between a 1/4 or 1/8 turn to the right.

6. When properly positioned, the bass can be supported between the left leg and groin.

Playing position. The conditions listed for establishment of the playing position for the cello (p. 11) apply equally to the string bass, with the following exceptions (see Figures 1-30 through 1-32):

1. Because of the longer string, length, the fingers should be spread wider apart.

2. Elbow position will be angled away from the body more than the 45° angle for the cello.

Figure 1–30. Correct playing position.

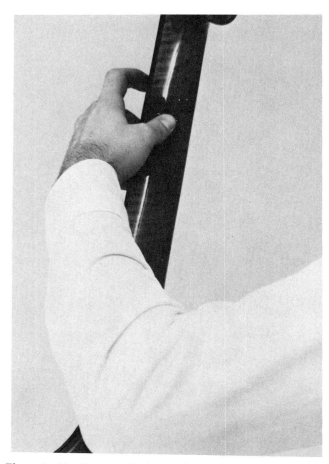

Figure 1–31. Correct playing position.

3. The left wrist may be bent slightly above the plane of the forearm and hand.
4. The thumb will be set about 7 inches from the nut.

Common errors

1. The instrument is perpendicular to the floor.
2. The student is too far behind the instrument.
3. The wrist is collapsed and the palm touches the neck of the instrument.
4. The thumb is opposite the first finger.
5. The elbow droops toward the body.

First Playing Exercises—Open Strings—Pizzicato

All first approaches to sound production should be introduced through the use of pizzicato. The use of pizzicato offers the following advantages:

1. Compared to playing with the bow (arco), there is relatively little right-hand motion to keep under control.

Figure 1–32. Compare the position of the thumb and fingers between the correct left-hand playing position (Figures 1–30 and 1–31) and this incorrect illustration.

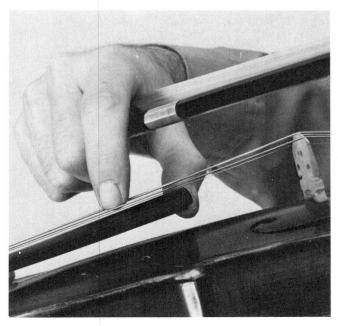

Figure 1–33. Pizzicato position for violin and viola.

2. Pizzicato allows the student to focus more attention on the establishment of individual concepts while producing sound: posture and body attitude, left-hand and left-arm position, support of the instrument, etc.

3. Pizzicato is the most immediate technique for getting your class involved in the process of sound production.

4. When finger placement and finger patterns are being established (Chapter 2), use of pizzicato will not interfere with the object of achieving the proper set of the left hand—while the use of the bow could.

Figures 1–33 through 1–35 illustrate the most common positions of the right hand for pizzicato. The use of pizzicato while holding the bow, however, should not be introduced until your students have gained an adequate command of the bow grip (next section).

The following points should be observed when introducing pizzicato:

1. The right thumb is firmly anchored on an appropriate position on the fingerboard.

2. The right wrist should be flat, with an imaginary straight line from the top of the forearm to the large knuckles.

3. The string is pulled *across* the fingerboard with the pad of the index finger in a slight lifting motion. The lifting motion at the end of the pizzicato cycle allows the finger to clear the string and places it in a more favorable position for succeeding articulations.

Figure 1–34. Pizzicato position for cello and French bass bow.

Figure 1–35. Pizzicato position for French bass bow.

EXERCISE 1–1

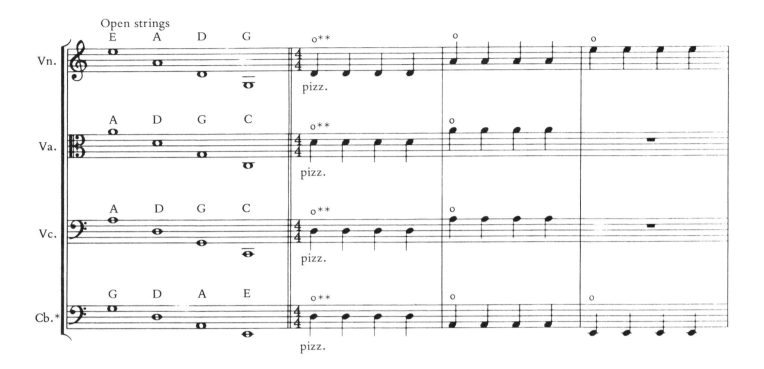

*String bass sounds one octave lower than written.   **Indication for open strings.

Steps to Holding the Bow

This phase of instruction should begin with *all* students in the sitting position—instruments in cases and away from the playing area. Do not complicate the students' learning the bow grip and attempting to manipulate the bow, with their struggling to keep their instruments at a rest position. Here are some of the advantages of teaching the bow grip with the students in the sitting position:

1. If the bow is accidentally dropped, the chance of damage to it is less than if they were standing.
2. Students can rest the tip of the bow on the left forearm (after the following preparatory exercises) and adjust their fingers, yet feel secure about the grip. This will also prepare the students for the eventual transfer of the bow to the instrument.

Before you begin to teach the bow grip, demonstrate the correct way to take the bow out of the case. This is especially necessary when working with children. Show them how to move the frog clamp, lift the frog, and then slide the tip of the bow out of its protector. Follow the reverse order when returning the bow to the case. For the cello and bass covers, point out that the tip of the bow is always inserted into the pouch first. In this way, only the frog is handled. As a further precaution, remind your cello and bass students that the bow is always the *first out* and *last in* when the instrument comes with a canvas cover. At this point, it will be helpful to review the points listed in "Working plan," p. 5.

Preparatory position. When your students understand the proper way for handling the bow, ask them to take their bows from their cases, then direct them through the following steps:

1. Place the bow across the lap with the frog to the student's left and hair toward the student.
2. Ask your students to dangle the *right* hand at the right side of the chair, encouraging them to wiggle their hands until they feel totally relaxed.

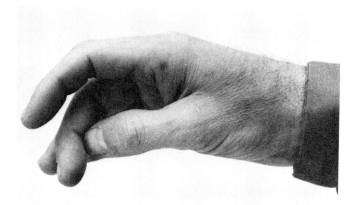

Figure 1–36. Intersection of thumb and middle finger.

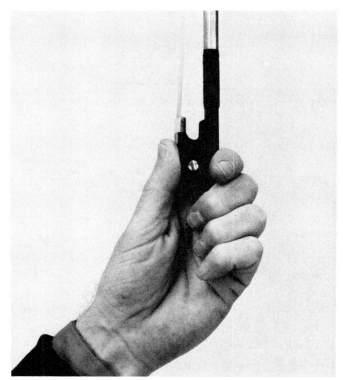

Figure 1–37

3. With the hand relaxed and at rest at their sides, let the *students* point out the shape or position of the totally relaxed hand: fingers slightly curved, wrist and forearm straight in an unbroken line from the mid-forearm to the knuckles, outside of the hand—from the wrist to the fingertips—shaped like a backward letter *J*, thumb knuckle slightly out, and middle fingers close to each other. The correct "set" of the bow grip stems from this natural and relaxed position; and there should be little if any difference between the bow grip and the hand in its relaxed position. During the early stages of holding the bow, this step should be repeated frequently to insure that the hand remains in this relaxed position.
4. With the hand still in the relaxed position, bend the thumb until it is opposite the second finger.* Move the second (middle) finger toward the thumb until the first crease of this finger intersects the thumb nail (see Figure 1–36). Encourage students to memorize this sensation. They can now raise their hands and take a close-up look at the preparatory position. Again, ask them to describe the shape and position of the hand and fingers.
5. Pick up the bow with the *left* hand, grasping it firmly with the turn screw, and stick it into the folds of the first two fingers. Place the tip of the *left* thumb

* Fingers are numbered consecutively from 1 to 4 beginning with the index finger as 1.

Figure 1–38. Contact point for hand in Figure 1–40.

Figure 1–39. Contact points for hand in Figure 1–41.

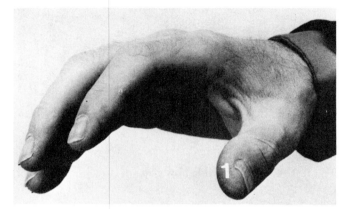

Figure 1–40

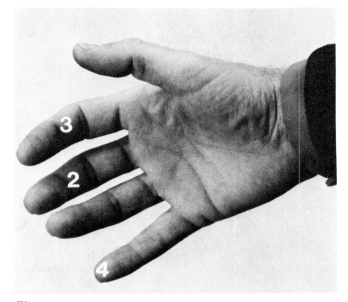

Figure 1–41

on the frog heel just below the slide. Point the tip of the bow toward the ceiling with the hair facing the student, and rotate the bow a little to the left—about 1/8 of a turn (see Figure 1–37).

Contact points. The contact points for the French-style bow are illustrated in Figures 1–38 and 1–39. The corresponding contact points for the right hand are given in Figures 1–40 and 1–41.

With the exception of the cello and bass bows, the first three contact points are common to all bows. For the cello and bass grips, the fourth contact point is slightly different. The first crease of the little finger—*not* the tip—and the side of the stick—*not* the top— are the corresponding contact points.

Explain to your class how these points are joined when establishing the bow grip.

Violin/Viola Bow Grips

With the bow in the position of Figure 1–37, raise the right hand in its relaxed position—with the wrist and forearm still forming a straight, unbroken line—until the forearm is parallel to the floor. Proceed as follows:

1. With the thumb quite bent, place the right corner of the tip of the thumb (contact point 1) on the *stick* between the edge of the frog and end of the winding (thumb grip). The center of the thumb should rest against the corner of the frog. In the early stages, the thumb cuticle should touch the bow hair. This is to insure that it is sufficiently bent. Later, when the grip begins to set, the thumb may be straightened

slightly away from the hair. The amount of bend will vary with the length of the thumb and the shape of the hand. Keeping the knuckle even slightly bent allows the thumb to set as a natural spring; a straight or flat thumb will be "locked," causing stiffness and inhibiting certain bow articulations.

2. Drop the second finger over the top of the stick (opposite the thumb) with the tip of the finger fairly close to the corner of the ferrule. The top of the stick should rest in the first crease of the second finger—contact point 2. The third finger is placed over the top of the stick next to the second finger.

3. Place the first finger over the winding of the stick, with the stick running between the two creases of the finger. Leave a slight space between the first and second fingers, between contact points 2 and 3.

4. Keeping the fourth finger in its naturally arched position, place the tip of the finger on the top of the stick—close to, but not touching the third finger—contact point 4. *Do not allow students to place their fourth fingers on the turn screw button.*

Except for the bending of the thumb and second finger, the hand on the bow should still have the same general shape as the relaxed preparatory position. When all fingers are in position, the left hand should be removed from the

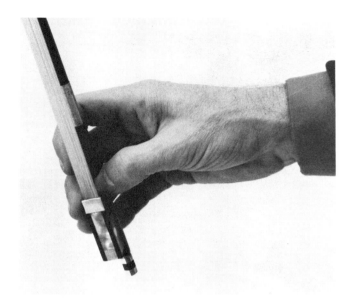

Figure 1–42. Violin/viola bow grip.

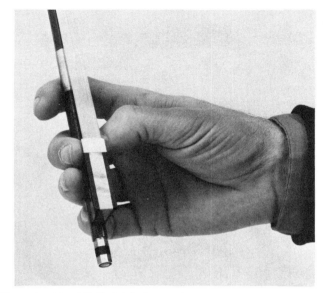

Figure 1–43. Violin/viola bow grip.

Figure 1–44. Violin/viola bow grip.

frog. The students can now rotate the bow and set the tip on their left forearms, keeping the bow almost parallel to the floor. Figures 1–42 through 1–44 illustrate an acceptable violin or viola bow grip.

Cello Bow Grip

With the bow in the preparatory position (Figure 1–37), raise the right hand in its relaxed position—with the wrist and forearm still forming a straight, unbroken line—until the forearm is parallel to the floor. Proceed as follows:

1. With the thumb slightly bent, place the right corner of the tip of the thumb on the stick between the edge of the frog and end of the winding—contact point 1.
2. Drop the second finger over the stick (opposite the thumb) until the pad of the finger touches the edge of the ferrule. The top of the stick should rest in the first crease of the second finger—contact point 2.
3. Place the first finger over the winding of the stick with the stick running between the two creases of the finger. Leave a slight space between the first and second fingers, between contact points 2 and 3.
4. Drop the third finger over the stick with the pad resting on the edge of the frog—but not under it.
5. Unlike the little finger in the violin and viola bow grip, the fourth finger on the cello bow *does not* rest on the top of the stick. The fourth finger is extended over the stick with the tip of the finger almost covering the pearl eye. Depending on the length of the fourth finger, the stick may rest in the first crease of the little finger or slightly higher. Figures 1–45 and 1–46 illustrate two views of an acceptable cello bow grip.

String Bass Bow Grip

French bow. With the preparatory position of Figure 1–37, raise the right hand in its relaxed position—with the wrist and forearm still forming a straight, unbroken line—until the forearm is parallel to the floor. Proceed as follows:

1. With the thumb slightly bent, place the right corner of the tip of the thumb on the stick between the

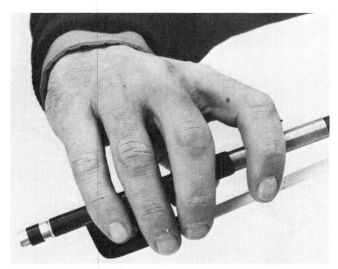

Figure 1–45. Cello bow grip.

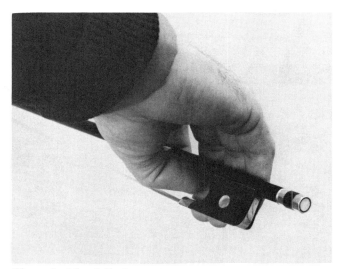

Figure 1–46. Cello bow grip.

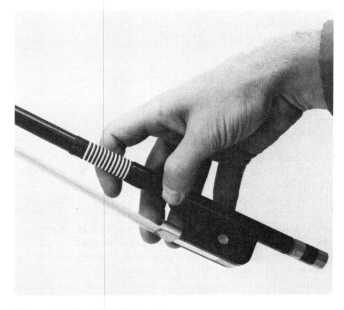

Figure 1–47. French bass bow grip.

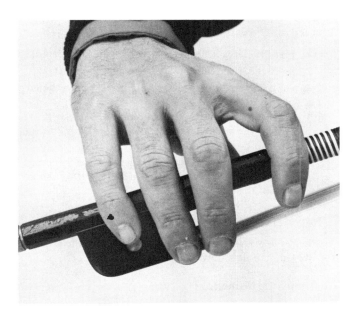

Figure 1–48. French bass bow grip.

edge and the end of the winding. The center of the thumb should rest against the corner of the frog—contact point 1.

2. Place the second finger over the stick and opposite the thumb. The pad of the finger tip should rest against the edge of the ferrule. The top of the stick should rest just above the first crease of the second finger. The third finger is placed over the top of the stick slightly to the right of the second finger.

3. Set the first finger over the winding so that the stick lies between the two creases of the finger. The first finger should be well forward of the thumb and curved over the stick.

4. Drop the fourth finger over the stick, placing the pad of the tip of the finger on the pearl eye. Depending on its length, the fourth finger will rest on the first joint or slightly higher, toward the second joint. There should be a slight spread between all fingers, especially between the first and second fingers. Figures 1–47 and 1–48 illustrate an acceptable bow grip for the French bass bow.

German bow. With the left hand, hold the bow at the center of the stick, keeping it parallel to the floor. The frog should be to the right side and the hair toward the floor.

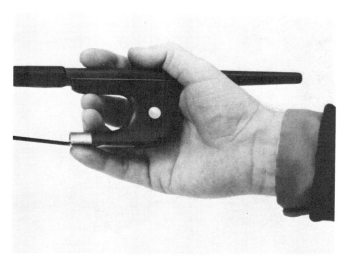

Figure 1–49. German bass bow grip.

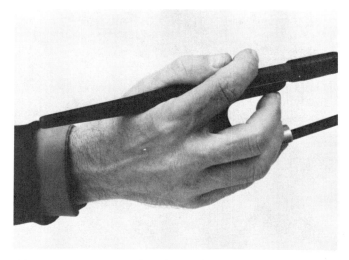

Figure 1–50. German bass bow grip.

Proceed as follows:

1. Place the bow screw in the web of the right hand.
2. Arch the thumb and place it on top of the stick.
3. Arch the fourth finger and place the tip on the edge of the ferrule.
4. With the first finger slightly curved, place it on the side of the stick. The tip of the thumb should touch the first crease of the first finger.
5. Place the second finger along the first, keeping it slightly curved. The tip of the second finger should rest on the top edge of the frog.
6. Bend the third finger and allow it to rest in the curve of the frog.

Figures 1–49 and 1–50 illustrate an acceptable bow grip for the German bass bow.

An Alternative Method

As an alternative, you can introduce the bow grip using a pencil instead of the bow. There are several advantages to this approach:

1. The pencil feels similar to the stick but has none of the disadvantages of controlling the weight and balance of the bow.
2. The pencil grip exposes the interior of the hand for easy examination.
3. The hand can be turned more freely to many angles of view.
4. It avoids accidents that can occur to the bow during the introductory stages of learning the grip.
5. General visibility of the contact points, as well as the shape and position of the fingers and thumb, is greater.

A dowel rod can be substituted for pencils (8 inches

long), allowing you to mark contact points with numbers, letters, or even colors. The following diameters are recommended:

Violin/viola: 3/8 inch
Cello: 1/2 inch
Bass: 5/8 inch

Summary of the Bow Grip

The bow grip is derived from the natural position of the totally relaxed hand and is characterized by a general roundness. The overhang of the fingers on the bow is relative and depends on the length of the fingers and general shape of the hand. Any deviation from the natural curvature of the fingers and correct placement of the fingers on the contact points must be corrected quickly. Once the hand begins to set into a grip—even incorrectly—it becomes habit. Reestablishing the proper grip can be very difficult. Take sufficient time to review the preparatory steps and finger placement before introducing newer concepts.

Common Errors in the Bow Grip

The following is a listing of the common errors that students tend to make in the early stages of holding the bow:

1. Fourth finger on turn screw button
2. Thumb on frog, not on stick
3. Straight or flat fourth finger
4. All fingers straight—knuckles up
5. Thumb bent in instead of out
6. Pad of thumb on stick—not tip—or thumb extending through the bow grip.
7. First finger well beyond the second crease
8. Middle fingers (second and third) too high up on the stick and/or third and fourth fingers off the stick

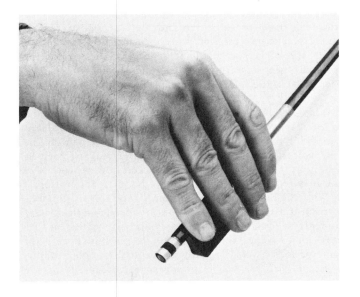

Figure 1–51. Incorrect bow grip: violin and viola.

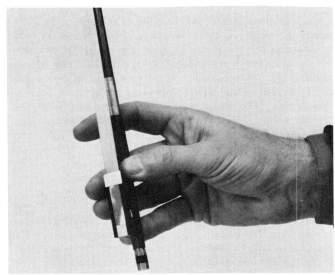

Figure 1–52. Incorrect bow grip: violin and viola.

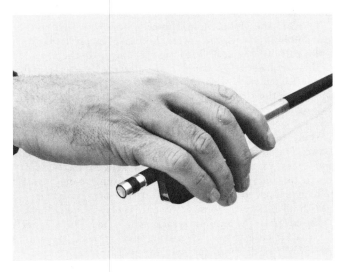

Figure 1–53. Incorrect cello bow grip.

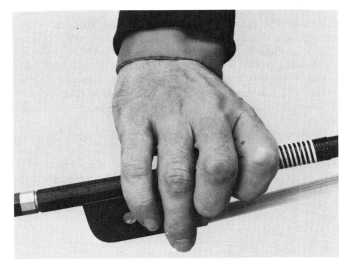

Figure 1–54. Incorrect French bass bow grip.

9. Fingers too far apart or too close together
10. Cello: top of stick slipping under the large knuckle of the little finger
11. German bass bow: frog heel against the palm of the hand

Several of these errors are illustrated in Figures 1–51 through 1–54.

TIGHTENING AND ROSINING THE BOW

A string teacher is often asked, "How much should I tighten my bow?" and "How much rosin should I use?"

An *exact* answer to either question cannot be given because of a number of variables: resiliency of the stick, condition and amount of bow hair, type of rosin, and effects of weather, just to mention a few. The experienced string player knows these variables, but will also consider the playing characteristics of the instrument when tightening and rosining the bow.

The new student learns these adjustments primarily through trial and error. But there are certain telltale clues to look and listen for when either amount (tautness or rosin) falls in or out of an acceptable range of application.

Tightening. When taught the general mechanical or physical properties of the bow, students will not only have a partial answer to the first question—"How tight?"—but also a better understanding of the function of the bow and how it generates sound in the instrument. Show the class that when the bow is correctly tightened, the hair and stick interact in two ways. First, the individual strands of hair flatten out and give the appearance of a smooth ribbon. Secondly, the curvature of the stick—which was achieved by heating and bending the wood—decreases slightly, distributing its tension evenly along the length of the hair. Both interactions allow the bow to produce a clear, resonant tone from frog to tip.

To demonstrate tightening, hold the bow in the *left* hand, grasping it very much like the bow grip, but with the thumb on the frog slide. This will help to minimize the wear between the turn screw shank and eyelet.

Because of the variables mentioned, it is misleading to tell students that one or two turns of the turn screw is sufficient to tighten (or loosen) the bow. When the bow is correctly tightened, the distance between the hair and the stick (at their closest points) is about a quarter inch for the violin bow and successively greater distances for viola, cello, and bass bows. Again, these distances are conditioned by the variables. The curved stick and flat, ribbonlike hair are, however, the main features to look for when checking for correct bow hair tension. Any deviation from these is easily recognizable. Once the students have gained some experience with basic bowing, they can test the "feel" of the bow by drawing it at a relatively high dynamic level. If the hair is too loose, it will touch the underside of the stick. When the bow is sufficiently taut, the bow will be responsive for a variety of dynamic demands and a wide range of articulations.

With the stick and hair under proper tension, the bow functions like a combination spring and shock absorber. Too much or not enough tension, and this dual function is lost. This is what can happen when either adjustment is excessive:

Too Loose

1. Fewer strands of hair are in contact with the string.
2. Hair touches underside of stick.
3. Full dynamic range of the instrument is impaired.
4. Loss of traction or "grab" at mid bow.
5. Damage to stick: warping.

Too Tight

1. Spring and shock-absorbing effect are lost.
2. Bow will bounce or "stutter."
3. Playing softly becomes difficult.
4. Area of contact with the string is decreased.
5. Damage to stick: loss of curvature.

When the bow is not in use, it must be loosened to a point where there is still a *slight* amount of tension in the stick and hair. Damage to the stick and hair will result if the bow is left in its taut adjustment: the curvature of the stick will begin to straighten and the hair will stretch excessively. The hair on a properly loosened bow should not touch the stick, nor should it hang loose away from the stick. Loosen it until several strands begin to separate. Viewed from the side, the hair appears to thicken.

Rosining. Before each use, the bow hair should be checked to see if rosin is needed. How much rosin to apply is determined by the condition and amount of bow hair. If the bow hair is worn or sparse, rosin will not cling to it as readily as it would on a freshly rehaired bow. A worn bow hair may require more rosin or more frequent applications.

With the hair in good condition, a good rule of thumb is to rosin it after each hour of *continuous* playing. Advising students to rosin before *each use* is a relative statement that can lead to some minor problems. If the bow is used for short periods, twenty minutes a day, for example, rosining it before *each use* will cause an excessive build-up on the hair, spreading rosin dust on the top of the instrument and fingerboard. The rosin will also cake on the strings and inhibit tone production—a frequent problem with children. They often go to the opposite extreme as well—no rosin at all. Their bows should be checked periodically.

To rosin the violin, viola, and cello bow hair, tighten the bow and hold it with the normal bow grip, or place the frog in the palm of the hand with the first finger on the top and parallel to the stick. With the hair perfectly flat, add a little weight to the stick with the first finger and draw the bow hair across the rosin in a straight line—from frog to tip and back again. Several back and forth strokes should be sufficient for one hour's playing.

When rosining the bass bow, use a slightly different procedure. The bow is held as above, but because of the softer consistency of bass rosin, the bow is pulled *quickly* from frog to tip *only*—never back and forth. Doing so may cause the hair to stick to the rosin and stretch or break the hair.

With all bows, it is best at first to apply rosin gradually to the hair until the amount is satisfactory. It is much easier to add a bit later than to overrosin, in which case it cannot be removed easily from the hair and will just have to wear away.

At this point, a few precautionary measures should be mentioned:

1. Whether using the circular-cake or block-type rosin, the student must not "saw" into the rosin. Show them how to rotate the circular cake or adjust the block when drawing the hair over the entire surface. In this way the rosin will wear down evenly and last for many years. If it is not rotated or adjusted, the rosin will become grooved and eventually crack. Do not allow broken pieces of rosin to accumulate in the case.
2. After each use, wipe rosin dust from the stick, instrument, and strings with a clean, soft cloth.
3. Fingers should never touch the bow hair. The oils from the fingers are quickly absorbed by the bow hair and dissolve some of the rosin, leaving a slick spot.

Preliminary Bow Exercises

The following exercises are performed with the correct bow grip and may be used as daily warm-ups. Their purpose is to help the student gain confidence in holding the bow, while exercising fingers, wrist, and arm. The titles are suggestions only and are offered to simplify the distinctions between them.

1. *Windshield wiper.* With the tip up, move the bow from left to right and back again, feeling the weight of the bow shifting between the first and fourth fingers. Here the bow pivots on the thumb with the first and fourth fingers being the most active of the moving parts. A variation on this exercise can be accomplished by keeping the fingers, hand, wrist, and forearm as a single unit—rotating it—with the pivotal action in the elbow.

2. *Push-ups.* Support the bow tip on the left forearm. Flex the fingers so that they are alternately straight then "curved" over the stick. The "curved" position is the regular bow grip.

3. *Waves.* Hold the bow at eye level and parallel to the floor, and move it from side to side describing the following pattern: ⌒⌒⌣ Let the wrist act like a hinge to form the up and down cycles of the pattern.

4. *Drum major.* With the tip up, flex the wrist and fingers, raising and lowering the bow in a perfectly straight line. The fingers will be straight at the lowest point—curved at the highest.

5. *Ovals.* Hold the bow at eye level and parallel to the floor. Draw the bow in a counterclockwise motion. Start with a circle, then gradually decrease the curvature of the pattern to form a flat oval (ellipse): from ◡ to ◡ to ◠.

6. *Soldier.* Place bow upside down on the left shoulder, fingers on the frog slide, thumb on the stick. Draw the bow down and up in a straight line. Drawing it perfectly straight can be done only if the wrist and elbow are allowed to hinge.

At first, some of these exercises may be too difficult for young students just learning to hold the bow. Should this be the case, it is advisable that they support the bow on the left forearm or on the instrument—in the preparatory position—until they feel more secure with the bow grip.

SOUND PRODUCTION AND TONE CONTROL*

Success with the beginning string class rests largely on how soon students can play with a pleasing tone and how well they understand the principles that govern tone production and control.

---

*The term "sound" is used here to refer to the basic or fundamental sound of the instrument, while "tone" refers to how it may be modified: dynamics, duration, articulations, etc.

The interdependence of both hands in producing and controlling tone is obvious, but teachers of string instruments soon discover that the development of the right hand is a greater challenge to the new student than acquiring the basic left-hand technique. While the left hand contributes two very important parts to the total quality of the sound (correct intonation** and vibrato), the right hand (bow) controls an almost unlimited variety of articulations and nuances of tone. In the early stages of instruction, considerable emphasis should be placed on discussion of and exercises for producing and controlling tone. When students understand how sound is produced and the factors that control it, they will in effect become self-instructive, diagnosing and correcting their errors. With this knowledge, their rate of assimilation and progress is greater, and their success sooner.

Sound Production

The surface of the bow hair, as you will recall, is not smooth but has minute irregularities that hold the rosin particles. When the bow is tightened, the hair and rosin combine to form a sandpaperlike ribbon. Without getting too technical, explain to the class that when the bow is pulled across the string, the rough edges of the hair pull the string off center—out of its state of rest. Show that because of the thickness and tension of the string, it can be pulled off center only a specific amount before it slips on the particles of rosin holding it and elastically snaps back—only to be caught again by other particles. Explain that this cycle of catches and releases is repeated as many times per second as the acoustical properties of the string will permit. This back and forth (periodic) motion creates the basic frequency of the string: 440 cycles per second (cps) for the violin A string, for example.

The vibrating string alone cannot produce a very audible sound or the sound we characterize as the "string" tone. The characteristic sound is created when the vibrating string sets off a chain reaction of other vibrating elements in the instrument: bridge, top, soundpost, bass bar, back, and sides. With all parts vibrating, the air in and around the instrument resonates, sympathetically reinforcing the basic frequency of the string. When the violin A string is bowed, for example, the 440 cps frequency will emerge as the most prominent pitch, but the *total* sound of the A is actually a composite of many frequencies, because each element (string, bridge, etc.) vibrates differently and contributes those *harmonics* that give the string instrument its unique sound.

The basic sound of the instrument can be changed only in pitch—when the string length is shortened by pressing it against the fingerboard with a finger of the left hand, or by vibrato. However, it can also be modified by articulations of the bow: changes in quality, duration, and dynamic levels. The way students control the bow often predicts

---

**Intonation as a factor in tone production is discussed in Chapter 2.

how quickly they will succeed in playing with a pleasing tone.

Tone Control: Factors

Although the instrument and bow are equals in the production of the basic sound, the bow is the dominant partner in controlling the tone. Controlling the tone of a string instrument has parallels with other instruments. The bow and right hand are in many ways similar to the embouchure and breath of the wind player, for example. To this extent, tone is more a property of the bow—and its control is reflected in the sound of the instrument. If the tone is not pleasing, the fault does not lie in the instrument, but in an incorrectly controlled bow; that is, the bow is actually interfering with the free vibration of the string and instrument. Once the student understands how the bow and instrument interact, the "mystery" of beautiful tone vanishes and there can be no reason for anything but a pleasing tone.

Beautiful tone production is governed by how well the bow's physical/mechanical principles are understood, applied, and controlled. With this knowledge, imperfections in tone production are easily diagnosed and corrected.

Physically, the bow is a wedge-shaped lever of disproportionate weight and point of balance. Naturally, it is heaviest at the frog and lightest at the tip. Its balance point is not at the middle, but slightly forward of the winding. The correct bow grip compensates for this by shifting the control of weight and balance into the hand. The bow, correctly held, pivots like the board of a teeter-totter, with the thumb serving as the fulcrum (see Figure 1–55). Weight can now be shifted to any point along the length of the stick by increasing or decreasing the weight of the first or fourth fingers. The first version of the "Windshield wiper" exercise given on p. 25 helps to establish this concept. Once this idea is understood, the factors that control the bow in *motion* can be introduced. When introducing the following factors, demonstrate the correct sound—defining all concepts very carefully and thoroughly before and during the demonstration.

Factors. When the bow is pulled across the string, several mechanical factors must be controlled to sustain or modify the basic sound of the instrument. The factors are placement, speed or pacing, weight, direction, and tilt. In early application of these factors, some are more or less constant—direction, placement, and tilt—while others are variable or graduated—speed and weight. These factors are isolated in the following paragraphs for the purpose of analysis and discussion; but in producing and controlling tone, they are interdependent and operate simultaneously.

Placement. The point at which the bow hair contacts the string—between the bridge and end of the fingerboard—controls the acoustic characteristics of the string and, in one way, the dynamic level of the tone. A full and brilliant sound results when the bow is played nearer the bridge; when it is played near the fingerboard, the tone is softer and more transparent. Because the instruments have different string lengths, each will have a correspondingly different point of bow placement. Violinists, for example, will not bow in the same area as bassists. This can be demonstrated by drawing the bow at different points between the bridge and fingerboard, determining at what point there is maximum dynamic response. Students will soon discover that the violin will be most responsive when played more toward the bridge side; the viola, midway between the bridge and fingerboard; cello and bass, from middle to fingerboard side. Bow placement over these contact points can be stated only generally because of the individual differences in the response characteristics of the instruments and bows. But with a little experimentation, the best contact points are soon discovered.

In the early stages of playing, the bow hair should be over the contact points that result in a full—yet pleasing—tone. The advanced player, however, will shift the bow placement over different contact points. Where the bow is placed depends on dynamic level and string length.

There are acoustic properties that govern the vibrating string and bow placement. As a general rule of thumb, the bow should be placed closer to the bridge side as the string length becomes shorter. This is obvious when comparing the location of bow placement for the open strings of the violin to those of the string bass. But the rule also applies when the string is shortened by the fingers of the left hand. The very high pitches that are created by the shorter string lengths bring the remaining string lengths closer to the fingerboard. If the bow is placed midway between the bridge and fingerboard on an inside string, the tone will not only be weak, but because the string is now closer to the fingerboard, the bow may also come in contact with the adjacent string. To correct this, the bow placement should be more toward the bridge side.

Tilt. For violin and viola, the stick is either tilted slightly toward the fingerboard or is directly above the bow hair. For cello and string bass, it is the general rule to tilt the stick toward the fingerboard.

When the dynamic levels of *pp* or *ppp* are indicated, it is sometimes necessary to tilt the stick of the bow more toward the fingerboard with as little hair as possible in contact with the string. However, this is an exaggerated bow position that alters the bow grip and should be reserved for the very softest dynamics only. The softest level can also be achieved with more bow hair (less tilt) by controlling other factors: bow placement closer to the fingerboard, or decreased weight and speed for example.

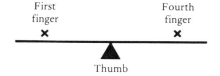

Figure 1–55.

Direction. To produce maximum tone and control, the bow must move at a right angle to the string—parallel to the bridge. With the bow moving in a perfectly straight line across the string, the hair has maximum traction, allowing the string to vibrate freely from side to side. In advance playing, subtle nuances or shadings of tone can be achieved by deliberately changing the angle of direction slightly at the tip or frog. But at the beginning stages, developing a direction that is perfectly straight must be the prime objective.

Speed. By controlling how quickly the bow moves from frog to tip (or the reverse), the player can alter the dynamic characteristic of the tone. Even with the natural weight of the bow alone, moving it faster produces a louder sound; slower, a softer sound. Graduation of speed will create the graduated dynamics of the crescendo, diminuendo, etc.

The control of speed and weight (the final factor) are the two most important bowing techniques. While placement, tilt, and direction are fairly constant factors, speed and weight are subject to the greatest amount of deliberate variations. In the course of drawing the bow, the player will consciously adjust the speed and weight of the bow to achieve the balanced tonal quality desired. All other factors must be correct, but speed and weight assume the dominant role in tone production.

Weight.* To make the bow equally responsive in all parts, its natural weight must be counterbalanced by weight from the right hand. The natural weight has to be equated by hand weight because of the concentration of natural weight in the areas of the frog, with its center of gravity somewhat forward of the winding.

When you draw the bow from frog to tip, for example, the point of maximum weight (frog) is moving away from the point of string contact, producing a slight decrescendo—from tip to frog, a crescendo. To maintain a dynamically balanced tone, weight is gradually added to the stick with the first finger or subtracted with weight to the fourth finger. For the German bass bow, weight is controlled by the thumb and web of the hand. Weight is increased by a slight counterclockwise rotation of the forearm and hand, transferring more weight to the thumb.

Figure 1–56 illustrates how finger weight compensates for bow weight when balancing the tone dynamically.

Again the "teeter-totter" principle is quite obvious: addition of weight is shifted between first and fourth fingers, with the thumb acting as the pivotal point. Under normal playing conditions, the first finger is more active as a counterbalancing weight than the fourth. The fourth finger becomes more active in advanced bowing techniques. Weight is also an important factor when playing on the lower, thick strings. Because they offer more resistance than the higher, thinner strings, more weight is required. This is es-

---

*The term *weight* is used in place of *pressure* to minimize the transfer of the latter term into feelings of tension or tightness that could result in grasping, squeezing, or clutching the bow.

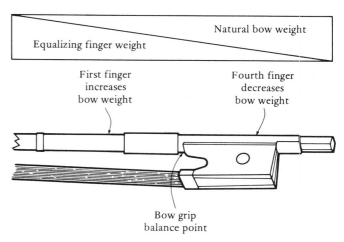

Figure 1–56

pecially true when maintaining a balanced sound while crossing from string to string.

Weight may be added to the bow by simply increasing the weight of the first finger *or* by a slight counterclockwise rotation of the forearm. This rotation will tip the balance of the hand into the first finger, transmitting the weight into the bow. Each technique results in the same outcome: increased weight.

Balancing the Factors—Errors in Tone Control

With the exception of incorrect left-hand finger placement on the fingerboard, most problems of tone control are directly related to improper control of one or more of the five factors. When there are errors in tone control, bow placement and tilt are not usually responsible. Correct application of placement and tilt is acquired sooner because these apply more to bow position than to bow motion. Tone control is most affected where the factors of direction, speed, and weight (aspects of motion) are concerned.

Bowing other than parallel to the bridge, and a disproportionate balance between bow speed and weight, are the main reasons for unsatisfactory tone. While bow direction is the least variable of the three, speed and weight are the main factors in balancing tone.

Once the students understand that beautiful tone is controlled by the interaction and balance of all factors, problems in tone production and control are more easily eliminated. If their tone production is less than satisfactory, it is an indication that the interaction and balance of the factors are either not thoroughly understood, or incorrectly applied. Assuming that the bow has the proper amount of tension and rosin, Table 1-1 presents a few examples of the effect on the tone quality and control when the factors are incorrectly applied.

In guiding the student toward attaining a beautiful tone, considerable emphasis should be placed on controlling the five factors. In the early stages, the student should be encouraged to make a conscious effort to be aware of how all

TABLE 1-1. Errors in Tone Control.

Placement

too close to the bridge	metallic and scratchy tone
too close to the fingerboard	thin tone—effective for *pp* dynamic level only

Tilt

too much toward fingerboard	transparent tone; stick may touch string and interfere with its free vibration

Direction

not parallel to the bridge	tone quality changes at different parts of the bow; smooth connection between strokes becomes difficult

Speed

too slow	bow "chatter," too soft, satisfactory for *pp* dynamic only
too fast	"whistling" tone, too loud; bow hair slides off placement point

Weight

too heavy	raspy or scratchy quality
too light	uncontrolled bow "bounce," not a full, resonant sound

TABLE 1-2. Divisions of the Bow.

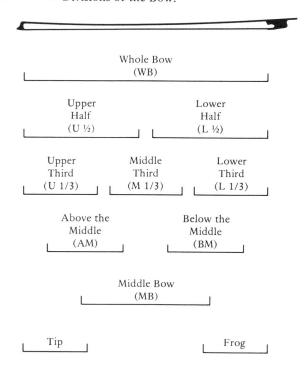

2. In orchestral playing, the conductor will use these terms (down-bow, at the frog, etc.) to achieve and unify the articulations and dynamics desired. These terms are the common language for communicating bowing between conductor and orchestra, and player to player.

factors are operating. With your help, they will soon gain control and begin to refine their application of the factors. As they advance, the factors will begin to function automatically; and when a variation in the use of one of the factors is necessary, it will be selective, not accidental.

BASIC BOWING

Division of the Bow

The bow has different response characteristics at different points along its length. Controlling all factors depends on what portion of the bow is in use and in what direction it is moving. The down-bow (⊓) is defined as the movement of the bow toward the tip; the up-bow (∨) as movement toward the frog. Explain the divisions of the bow before proceeding to the first bowing exercises. The most common divisions are illustrated in Table 1-2.

Memorize the symbols and abbreviations for the direction and divisions of the bow. They are important for the following reasons:

1. Some advanced bowing techniques can be executed only at specific parts of the bow; others with only one bow direction.

Bow Motion

Bow motion is coordinated through the interaction of the larger and smaller muscles, and joints in the bow arm. The amount of hinging and the specific muscles used are governed by the portion of the bow used, its speed, length, and the dynamic level required. In addition to these considerations, the bow factors (see pp. 26–28) must be integrated into overall bow movement. Bow motion may be divided into five separate categories, but each is truly dependent upon the others. The motions are essentially horizontal, vertical, or rotary:

1. *Shoulder:* involved in string crossings and playing with the lower portions of the bow.
2. *Upper arm:* most active when playing at the frog of the bow, in successive down-bow strokes, and in string crosses.
3. *Forearm:* controls most mid-bow playing, is used as a "middle" motion for whole-bow strokes, and often functions independent of the upper arm.
4. *Wrist:* cushions changes of bow direction.
5. *Fingers:* used for increases and/or decreases in bow weight, and for refining changes of bow direction.

Mechanics of Bowing

Mid-bow playing. * This stroke is initiated in the forearm, with the wrist on the same plane as the hand and forearm. There is little upper-arm motion, but a good deal of hinging at the elbow. Wrist and fingers may be involved to a greater or lesser degree at mid-bow playing, but the amount of movement is conditioned by the type of bow articulation. (See Chapter 5, "Bowing Techniques.")

Whole-bow playing. When this stroke is started at the frog, the wrist will be slightly above the plane of the hand and forearm. The bow motion is initiated in the upper arm, but as the bow reaches its midpoint, the wrist begins to flatten. The bow is kept parallel to the bridge by allowing the forearm to hinge at the elbow. From the middle of the bow to the tip, the wrist begins to lower slightly below the plane of the forearm and hand. The stroke is then completed with the forearm, wrist, and fingers. As the bow reaches the tip, there should be an increase of bow weight through the index finger to compensate for the decrease in natural bow weight. To perform this stroke beginning at the tip of the bow, the sequence of motions is exactly reversed.

Playing at the frog and tip. This type of playing requires greater use of the small muscles in the hand, wrist, and fingers. At the frog, natural bow weight must be counterbalanced by more wrist and finger motion. At this portion of the bow, there should be a feeling of elasticity and springiness in the hand and fingers. This feeling helps to cushion the changes of bow direction.

At the tip of the bow, for some articulation, the motion may be confined mainly to the fingers. In other articulations, there will be more of a combination of forearm, wrist, and finger motion. (See Chapter 5, "Bowing Techniques.")

Bow changes. The smooth connection between changes of bow direction at the frog and tip is controlled by the small muscles and joints in the wrist and fingers. At the middle portion of the bow the forearm and wrist movement connect the changes of direction. Because bow weight is naturally heavier at the frog, a smooth connection in this portion of the bow is achieved by slightly decreasing bow weight. The reverse is true for a smooth connection at the tip, slightly increasing bow weight.

The Basic Bow Stroke: Détaché

The basic bow stroke should be introduced when all factors, bow divisions, and direction have been thoroughly explained and demonstrated. *Détaché* (day-tah-**shay**) bowing as the name suggests, is used to play separate (detached) notes ♩ ♩, as opposed to connected (legato or slurred) notes ♩ ♩. That is, the bow changes directions for each new note: ♩ ♩.

*Also includes playing in the AM, BM, L 1/3, and U 1/3 portions of the bow.

Before actual bowing studies are begun, be sure to check the following points: (1) posture, (2) position of the instrument, (3) bow grip, (4) correct amount of tension and rosin for the bow, and (5) tuning of all instruments. In the beginning stages of bowing, the control of bow *direction* may be more troublesome than other factors. To move the bow parallel to the bridge, the bow arm should display the following characteristics:

Violin/viola. Motion is initiated and confined to the forearm only. The upper arm should not move and the shoulder should be relaxed. The wrist and elbow will act like hinges when drawing the bow parallel to the bridge. The "Soldier" exercise described on p. 25 will help to establish this motion.

Cello. Motion is initiated in the forearm with the upper arm in motion only to the point of retaining the straight bow. The elbow is more prominent as a hinge than the wrist, and the shoulder should be relaxed.

Bass. Motion is initiated in the entire arm with the shoulder joint acting as the primary hinge, elbow and wrist as secondary hinges.

When these characteristics are not present, the bow will describe an arc rather than a straight line. This results because the bow is being used as an inflexible unit—without hinges. Two things happen when the bow direction is not perfectly straight:

1. The hair, which is no longer at a right angle to the string, loses traction or grip of the string.
2. The bow slides toward the fingerboard for violin and viola, toward the bridge for the cello and bass.

First Bowing Exercises

With the left hand placed in the preparatory position—on the upper bout—proceed with the following rote exercises. To insure concentration, the rote approach should be used when introducing any new technique. Tell the students to:

1. Set the bow on the D string, above the middle of the bow (AM), and check the following: (a) Placement: the hair should contact the string midway between the bridge and end of the fingerboard; refinements of placement can take place when the basic bow stroke has been mastered. (b) Tilt: for violin and viola, the stick should be directly above the hair, or tilted only slightly toward the fingerboard; the tilt for the cello and bass bow is *always* slightly toward the fingerboard. (c) Shoulder and elbow: the shoulder should be relaxed; the elbow should be elevated enough to preserve the positions illustrated in Figures 1–57 through 1–59. The elbow should not sag toward the body; (d) Bow grips: the fingers should be rounded (curved) over the stick.
2. Add a small amount of *weight* to the bow with the

Figure 1-57. Basic violin and viola bowing position.

Figure 1-58. Basic cello bowing position.

Figure 1-59. Basic bowing position for the bass.

first finger so the stick bends slightly toward the hair, and proceed with Exercise 1-3.

3. Count off a measure of ♩ = 60 and *pull* the bow toward the tip (⊓), stopping it just below the point of the bow. Keep the hair "into" the string with the same *weight*. There should be a clean stop after each note. The rest provides time to plan out each move. Then *push* the bow in the direction of the frog (∨), returning it to the starting point of Step 1. Repeat this procedure several times so the factor of *bow direction* can be observed.

These procedures can now be repeated on the remaining strings—Exercise 1-4. To position the bow on a new string requires a different bowing *plane*. The feel of the plane is correct when the bow does not touch an adjacent string. The bow is moved to each new plane by raising or lowering the entire arm as a vertical unit, allowing it to pivot at the shoulder. In advanced playing, rapid string crosses--changes between planes--can be accomplished with little or no upper-arm involvement. Here the motion is confined to the hand and wrist.

EXERCISE 1–3

Practice points:
- Keep the bow on the string for each rest.
- Allow elbow and wrist to hinge naturally.

EXERCISE 1–4

Practice points:
- Keep the bow on the string for each rest.
- Raise or lower bow and upper arm *as a unit* to cross from string to string—do not raise right shoulder.

EXERCISE 1–5

Practice points:
- Use equal amounts of bow for each note.
- Allow elbow to act as a hinge, keeping bow motion centered in forearm.

EXERCISE 1–6

Practice points:
- Use equal amounts of bow for each note.
- Decrease bow weight for quarter notes.

When switching from *arco* to *pizz.*, the frog of the bow is pulled into the palm and held there by the second, third, and fourth fingers. This frees the thumb (to be anchored on the fingerboard) and the first finger. (See Figs. 1–33 to 1–35.)

EXERCISE 1–7

Practice points:
- Use equal amounts of bow for each note.
- Decrease bow weight on quarter notes.

EXERCISE 1–8

Practice points:
- Keep bow direction parallel to bridge from frog to tip.
- Allow wrist to hinge naturally as bow approaches frog or tip.

*See "whole-bow playing," p. 29.

EXERCISE 1–9

Practice points:
- Conserve bow speed at the beginning of each stroke.
- Add bow weight when approaching tip; decrease weight when close to frog.

EXERCISE 1–10

Practice points:
- Distribute bow length in relation to note length.
- Allow elbow and wrist to hinge naturally on quarter notes.

EXERCISE 1–11*

Practice points:
- Use equal amounts of bow for each note.
- Raise or lower bow and upper arm *as a unit* to cross from string to string.

EXERCISE 1–12*

Practice points:
- Use less bow for the eighth notes, but with increased bow weight.
- Raise or lower bow and upper arm *as a unit* to cross from string to string.

*Practice Exercises 1–11 and 1–12 three ways: 1) MB, 2) AM, 3) BM.

EXERCISE 1–13*

Practice points:
- Distribute bow length in relation to note length.
- Raise or lower bow and upper arm *as a unit* to cross from string to string.

EXERCISE 1–14*

Practice points:
- Distribute bow length in relation to note length.
- Raise or lower bow and upper arm *as a unit* to cross from string to string.

*Practice Exercises 1–13 and 1–14 three ways: 1) MB, 2) U 1/3, 3) L 1/3.

EXERCISE 1–15*

Practice points:
- Keep bow on string for rests.
- Use equal amounts of bow for each note.

EXERCISE 1–16*

Practice points:
- Distribute bow length in relation to note length.
- Raise or lower bow and upper arm *as a unit* to cross from string to string.

*Practice Exercises 1–15 and 1–16 three ways: 1) MB, 2) tip, 3) frog.

TUNING THE INSTRUMENTS

First attempts at playing a string instrument must not be frustrated by an out-of-tune instrument; one whose pegs, tuners, or bass keys are not in perfect adjustment; or one with "false" strings (see Chapter 7). While playing on an in-tune instrument is the most important prerequisite to correct intonation, a perfectly tuned instrument is also more enjoyable to play because of its maximum resonance.

In the very first playing stages, and depending upon the age level of the students, the main responsibility for tuning the instruments will rest with the instructor. The least experienced students should have their instruments checked first and most frequently. Only in this way can they begin to develop the careful listening habits needed for accurate tuning. As students progress in the areas of instrument and bow control, pitch accuracy, and general information, they should be encouraged to develop tuning skills and assume more of this responsibility.

Tuning Sources

The A-440 frequency is the international tuning standard for musical instruments. It may be generated by a number of sources. Although the piano A-440 (the A above middle C) is by far the most common, its reliability as a comparison pitch is only as good as its tuning. The most accurate sources are the electronic tone generator, tuning bar, or tuning fork. An inexpensive and generally reliable source is the harmonica-type pitch pipe. Other than expense, it has the added advantage of portability. It can be carried in the instrument case, allowing the student to tune the instrument at home where other tuning sources might not be available.

When to Introduce Tuning

Once the class has had sufficient experience holding the instrument and playing with the bow, tuning procedures may be introduced. However, in the lower grades, physical limitations must be considered. And unless the violins, violas, and cellos of the youngest students are equipped with string tuners for each string, you will have to tune their instruments.

The readiness of the class for tuning can be demonstrated by asking them to sing the sound of the open strings (in their voice register) for their instrument. As a further verification of their pitch accuracy, sound the open strings of a slightly out-of-tune instrument, asking them to indicate the direction (higher or lower) the string must be adjusted to bring it into perfect tuning.

In addition to the above, the following information must be known or demonstrated by the students before you allow them to tune their instruments without assistance:

1. Names of the open strings, their designated pitches on the staff (and clef), and the location of their sounds on a piano keyboard or pitch pipe.

2. How the mechanical principles of the peg, tuner, and bass key operates—and which direction to turn the mechanism to make the string higher or lower.

3. Which string is wound onto which peg.

4. For the violin, viola, and cello, how to correctly rewind the string onto the peg if it slips off completely.

5. For the string bass, a reminder that the instrument sounds an octave lower than written, and that it is tuned in fourths.

Basic Principles of Tuning

While there are three different mechanical devices for tuning the strings, there are certain principles that apply to the tuning of all string instruments:

1. The string is most accurately tuned when the target pitch is *approached from below*. When tuning with the peg, it is first turned slightly toward the student, lessening the string tension and lowering the pitch. The peg is then turned *into* the peg box until the target pitch is reached. Tuning from below up to the target pitch will keep the string at its design tension.

2. Tuning with the bow, as opposed to pizzicato, provides a more reliable sound for comparison to the tuning A.

3. Except for the string bass, tuning with double stops (bowing on two strings simultaneously) is the ultimate verification of correct pitch. When the fifths between the strings are truly perfect, no secondary beats will be heard (see Chapter 7, "Care and Maintenance").

4. The tuning mechanism is turned only while the string is still vibrating—not after the sound has died away. Only in this way can the player determine how much of an adjustment is required to tune the string.

5. Tune with a light bow stroke at the upper half of the bow. One possibility is to tune up-bow only, lifting the bow from the string and listening to the sound as the tuning mechanism is turned.

6. Before turning the tuning mechanism, all strings should be checked to see if one is loose. Attempting to fine-tune a string without first correcting the loose one will result in wasted time because the combined string tension *across* the strings is not balanced. For example, if the A, E, and D strings of a violin are fine-tuned while the G is loose, when the G string is tuned it will change the pitch of the other strings and the entire tuning cycle will have to be repeated —needlessly.

Tuning the Violin, Viola, and Cello

In early instruction, fine tuning can be accomplished accurately and quickly with the string tuners. Accurate

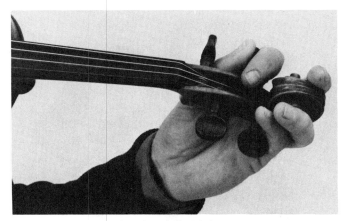

Figure 1–60. Turning the violin/viola pegs.

tuning with the pegs, however, requires more time to develop. When your students' fingers are strong enough to turn the pegs, and their pitch accuracy confirmed, demonstrate the principles of tuning with the pegs. The following procedures should first be introduced with your students holding their violins and violas guitar-style—plucking the strings with the right thumb while turning the pegs with the left hand.

Violin and Viola

Low Strings. Show them how to grasp the peg with the thumb and index finger while anchoring the middle and ring fingers around the scroll. The anchoring will provide the counterforce necessary when the peg is turned into the peg box (see Figure 1–60).

High strings. To tune the high strings, the thumb and middle fingers grasp the peg while the index finger is anchored on the side of the scroll (see Figure 1–61).

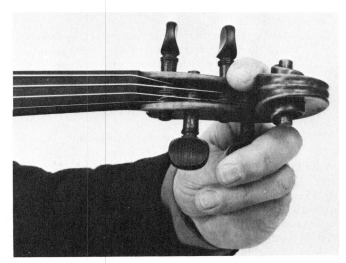

Figure 1–61. Turning the violin/viola pegs.

The highest string is always provided with a tuner; but should it have to be adjusted with the peg, the peg is grasped with the thumb and middle finger. The index finger is anchored between the pegs on the opposite peg box wall.

When students have developed some facility at turning the pegs while holding the instrument guitar-style, encourage them to try tuning the instrument in the playing position. The addition of the bow in the tuning process may be introduced after this intermediate phase.

Cello

Ask the cellists to turn their instruments around so that the strings are directly in front of them. The instrument must be stabilized with the left hand (see Figure 1–62).

High strings. Show them how to pluck the string with the thumb of the right hand—and while the string is still vibrating, reach up with the right hand and turn the peg into the peg box. If the peg does not hold, repeat the process holding the left hand on the opposite pegs for added counterforce (see Figure 1–63).

Low strings. Repeat the procedures described above, but with reversed left and right hands.

Figure 1–62. Turning the cello pegs (pizzicato).

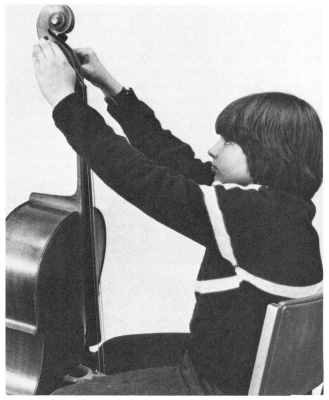

Figure 1–63. Turning the cello pegs (pizzicato).

Figure 1–64. Turning the cello pegs (playing position).

When the cello is tuned in the playing position, the counterforce is provided by the body: chest for the highest strings, left leg for the lowest strings (see Figures 1–64 and 1–65).

The addition of the bow in the tuning process may be introduced when your students can tune with the instrument in this position.

Tuning the String Bass

Although the bass possesses none of the physical and mechanical obstacles of tuning the violin, viola, and cello, the lowness of its strings makes pitch matching difficult. When the A-440 tuning standard is sounded, the bassist's open A sounds three octaves lower—A-55.

This problem is somewhat alleviated by the use of *harmonics* (see Chapter 5, "Natural and Artificial Harmonics") and by tuning with the bow. A harmonic is produced by placing the pad of the tip of the fourth finger lightly on the string (not touching the fingerboard) at one of its natural segments: one-half, one-quarter of the string length, etc. This allows the string to vibrate on either side of the point of finger contact. For example, placing the finger on the A string, midway between the fingerboard nut and the bridge, will produce a clear, flutelike sound that is one octave higher (A-110) than the open A. The sound is much more accessible as a comparison pitch. This

type of division of the string may serve as the introductory phase of harmonic tuning.

A second and more accurate type of harmonic tuning is achieved in the following way:

1. Start by placing the pad of the tip of the fourth finger lightly on the D string—a perfect fifth above the open string. The pitch produced should be the harmonic A-220— only one octave lower than the tuning standard.

2. Leaving the fourth finger in position on the D string, reach the first finger over to the A string and place it lightly on the string. If properly positioned, the harmonic produced will be in *unison* (A-220) with the D string harmonic. Adjust the A string tuning key to bring this harmonic in perfect unison with the D string.

3. Repeat this procedure to tune the remaining strings.

Minor Pitch Adjustments for Violin, Viola, and Cello

When a gut-wound string (no tuner) is only slightly sharp, its pitch can be adjusted by sliding the index finger of the right hand along the mid-portion of the string with a slight pulling motion. If the string does not respond quickly (lower), it should be retuned with the peg. If the string is only slightly flat, applying a little pressure to the string in

Figure 1-65. Turning the cello pegs (playing position).

the peg box—just above the fingerboard nut— may be sufficient. This last method is only a temporary expedient because the string tension will eventually pull the string flat. Eventually it will have to be retuned with the peg.

Tuning Procedures

The first string to tune for all string instruments is the A string. The accurate tuning of this string is critical because the pitches of the remaining strings will be eventually measured from it. To insure that the A string is accurately tuned, the tuning reference tone (A-440) must be sounded long and loud enough for the student to establish it as the comparison standard to match.

Matching the sound of the A string to the pitch of the tuning standard can be accomplished in the following sequence:

Pizzicato. While being the least reliable method for producing the comparison sound, pizzicato offers the most comfortable means for the beginning student. At first it is best to work with one student at a time, helping each to match the A string to the tuning standard. As the students become more self-reliant, the instruments may be tuned in sections:

violins, violas, etc. When bow management is well under control, the next method may be introduced.

Arco. Tuning with the bow produces a tone that is more easily compared to the tuning standard—not only because of its quality but also because the tone can be sustained. At first each string should be bowed and tuned individually, tuning adjacent strings: from A to D, D to G, etc.

Double-stops. Bowing and sustaining two adjacent strings allows the player to compare the quality of the interval produced. This type of tuning is the *most accurate*, because if the fifths between the strings for the violin, viola, and cello are not *perfect*, an interference pattern between the strings results in an acoustical phenomenon called *beats*. The beats indicate how far the string should be adjusted. The closer to perfect tune the string is adjusted, the slower the beating will be. When the beating stops, the interval of the fifth is *perfect*.

Alternate approaches. Two other methods—with varying degrees of acceptability—are listed below. Ultimately, you will have to determine which approach will be most successful for your class. Whatever approach is chosen, an organized routine must be developed.

One alternate method of tuning simply involves the matching of the sound of the open strings to the same pitches on a piano or pitch pipe. This type of tuning is suitable only at the beginning stages of tuning because it is based on *several* external reference pitches. Our desired goal is to help students to determine the pitches of the strings solely from the A-440 reference.

A final method requires that the student sing-hear the sound of the new strings after the A string has been tuned to the A-440 reference. This procedure is given below:

For violin, viola, cello: After matching the sound of the open A string to the sound of the tuning standard, tell your class to call this sound "5" and guide them through the singing of the major scale pattern 5-4-3-2-1. The "1" at the end of the pattern is the target pitch for the next *lowest* string: D. For the viola and cello, this cycle may be continued by calling all successively lower strings "5" and repeating the pattern 5-4-3-2-1. The sound of the open E for the violin can be found by reversing the pattern: 1-2-3-4-5.

For the string bass: The same procedure may be used starting with the tuned open A, calling it "1" and singing the major scale pattern 1-2-3-4. Here the "4" at the end of the pattern is the target sound for the next *highest* string: D. This pattern may be repeated by calling all successively *higher* strings "1" and repeating the pattern 1-2-3-4; The sound of the open E can be found by reversing the pattern: 4-3-2-1.

The process of tuning by harmonics—described on p. 40—is, however, the most accurate method for tuning the string bass.

Chapter 2

DEVELOPMENTAL EXERCISES: BASIC LEFT- AND RIGHT-HAND TECHNIQUES

A well-balanced string technique requires the development of a disciplined coordination between the mechanics of the left hand and motion of the right hand. While our aim is to integrate both concepts as soon as possible, this is not usually attainable at the very earliest stages of playing and teaching. Therefore, the two concepts are divided so that emphasis is first given to the development of the students' left hand. This takes first priority not only because the left hand has the total responsibility for creating pitch, but also the development of the bow arm must begin on a foundation of a secure left hand.

The developmental exercises are divided into two equal sections so that emphasis is balanced between left- and right-hand techniques:

Section I contains exercises for the development of finger patterns. These exercises are designed to set the position of the left hand as a *single unit* with the fingers and thumb functioning as parts of the whole hand.

Section II contains exercises combining finger patterns with basic bowing patterns. These exercises reinforce the set of the left hand and finger patterns, while introducing right-hand techniques. When students can hold their instruments and bows comfortably and correctly, and when their basic bow strokes are satisfactory, left-hand finger placement and patterns may be introduced.

SECTION I

Finger Patterns

A vast majority of *tonal* string music is playable using four basic finger patterns and their various combinations. The finger patterns are categorized by the location of the half-step(s) in a five-note scale (pentachord) beginning on an open string. The four basic finger patterns are illustrated in Figure 2–1. The $\vee$ shows the location of the half-step. Executing the complete sequence of Patterns III and IV usually requires the technique of shifting (on the same string) to a higher position (see Chapter 5).

Certain keys are more closely associated with string music than others because of the *finger patterns* they create. D major, for example, is a very common string key because the pitches in its scale (Pattern I) may be produced with the fingers and hand in the most relaxed position. The number of open strings in a given key is also important. Open strings permit maximum resonance of the instrument through sympathetic vibration, and provide a stable reference standard for verifying intonation. For these reasons, certain keys are frequently chosen when introducing *left-hand* techniques.

While setting and establishing any finger pattern, check the following points very carefully. Personal attention is extremely important at this time because the beginner forms habits very quickly. Without direct observation and individual attention, the habits established are more likely to be incorrect ones.

1. Correctly tuned instrument
2. Placement of the thumb on neck
3. Shape of fingers over the strings
4. Position of elbow in relation to the instrument
5. Position of the wrist in relation to the forearm and hand.
6. Relaxed left shoulder, arm, and hand

Finger Placement

In addition to the six preparatory check points just listed, there are some general procedures to consider when this phase of instruction is initiated:

Figure 2–1. Basic finger patterns.*

*Clefs and accidentals are omitted in this figure to simplify the illustration of the location of the half-steps in the pentachord.

Ear training. The importance of *early* ear training cannot be overemphasized. When finger placement and patterns are started, encourage students to find the location of a new note by anticipating its pitch—*hearing it before playing it.* Using an open string as a reference pitch, ask them to sing, hum, or whistle each new note before setting a finger in place. In this way the accuracy of the intonation can be verified. If an early ear training approach is not used, accurate pitch recognition and location cannot be developed. And students will form the habit of playing finger *numbers*—placing the correct finger down but not in relation to the correct pitch.

As part of the ear training, show students how to test any note against an open string of the same letter-name. These notes are either unisons or octaves, and the comparison is a simple and accurate procedure. When a note is the same letter-name as an open string, the students should also be encouraged to listen for the sympathetic vibration of the open string to verify the intonation.

A pitch that is perfectly in tune does not vibrate alone but sets into vibration other strings that bear a simple ratio in relation to the original pitch. If, for example, when first finger (A) on the G string is played on the violin, viola, and cello, the open A string will vibrate sympathetically if the stopped note is perfectly in tune, reinforcing the sound of the stopped note. This can be verified by playing the first-finger A slightly sharp or flat and noting how dull and lifeless it sounds without the help of the sympathetic vibration of the open strings.

Finger guides. As an aid for the very young beginner, thin strips of adhesive tape may be placed under the strings where the fingers would be set in Pattern I. The tapes will guide their fingers quickly and accurately in locating finger placement and pitches. Once their fingers are correctly oriented to the fingerboard, and they have had sufficient practice with the four basic finger patterns, the tapes may be removed.

Rote and pizzicato. To permit maximum focus on the placement of the fingers, left-hand concepts should be introduced with as much rote and pizzicato playing as is practical. To vary the pizzicato playing, the violins and violas may be held in the " rest " position (see Chapter 1, p. 7). In this manner, the student has a better view of the position of the thumb, hand, and fingers. For added variety, urge your students to improvise one-string pizzicato melodies using a given finger pattern.

Finger action and economy. When the fingers are arched properly over the strings, foster an action of dropping and lifting the fingers that is elastic and springlike—but relaxed. Any squeezing of the thumb or fingers will cause tension and inhibit the development of this action. Sufficient periods of rest should be included in the time devoted to finger placement and patterns.

There is a tendency among beginning students to place the finger on each note in a "piano" style—alternately dropping and lifting each finger for each note. Remind your students often that pitches may be created by *lifting* the fingers as well as dropping them. When the fingers are left in place on a string in an ascending passage, for example, they are in "reserve" should the passage reverse direction or contain a lower note on the same string. However, when the fingers are lifted, care must be taken to keep them over the strings so that they retain their correct arch and shape.

Aural/tactile development. Once the rote mechanics of a pattern are understood, looking at the fingerboard should be discouraged. Locating the placement of a finger must be developed from an *aural/tactile*—not visual—standpoint.

Illustrations and Symbols

Each finger pattern is illustrated with photographs for the correct position of the hand and fingers; fingerboard diagrams for the placement of the fingers; and music showing the pitches created.

Here is an explanation of the symbols and abbreviations used in the following exercises:

1. A finger number followed by a line (3 ——) indicates that the finger remains on the fingerboard for the duration of the line.

2. A half-step is indicated with the symbol (∨); all other adjacent intervals are whole-steps.

3. A ☐ on a line or space indicates a preparatory finger—of the same number—on an adjacent string. Here, the finger stops two strings simultaneously: the played note and the preparatory note.

4. Bow divisions and abbreviations are given on p. 28.

Finger Pattern I

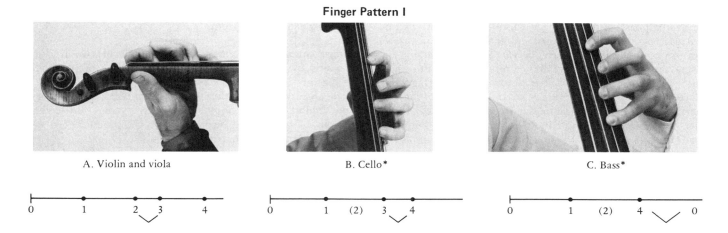

A. Violin and viola   B. Cello*   C. Bass*

The pitches created by Finger Pattern I are identical in sound to the first five notes in a *major* scale or the sequence *do-re-mi-fa-sol.*

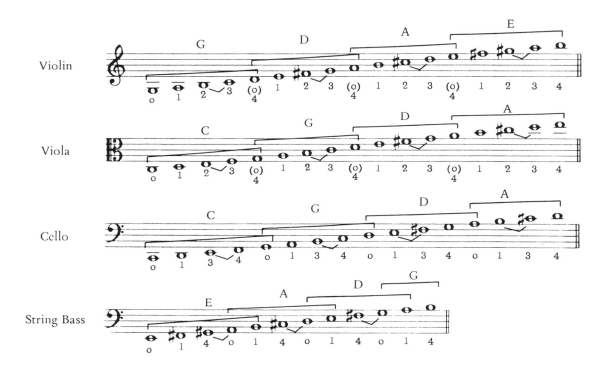

1. Keep your bow on the string during the rests and try to hear the pitch of each succcessive note before placing the fingers down.
2. Repeat Exercises 2–1 and 2–2 on the remaining strings.

*Although the placement of the second finger is not required to produce the pitches in this pattern, it is advisable to set *all* fingers down whether required or not.

44

EXERCISE 2-1

*t = Test the stopped note against the pitch of an open string of the same letter name.

EXERCISE 2-2

EXERCISE 2–3*

Practice points:
- Keep fingers down wherever possible.
- Whenever a finger is not in use, keep it poised over the fingerboard.

Practice points:
- Keep the left hand relaxed; do not squeeze.
- Keep the left elbow in its correct relation to the instrument.

*Before beginning exercises containing use of the whole bow (WB), it will be helpful to review the basic principles of "Bow Motion" and the "Use of the Whole Bow" Chapter 1, p. 28–29.

FROM *SYMPHONY NO. 9,* FOURTH MOVEMENT

Beethoven

*Original tempo indication is *Allegro*.

Finger Pattern II

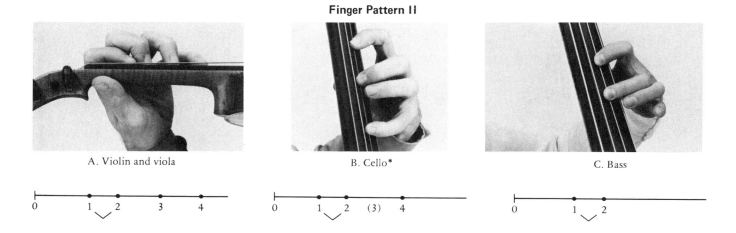

A. Violin and viola   B. Cello*   C. Bass

The pitches created by Finger Pattern II are identical in sound to the first five notes in a *minor* scale or the sequence *la-ti-do-re-me*.

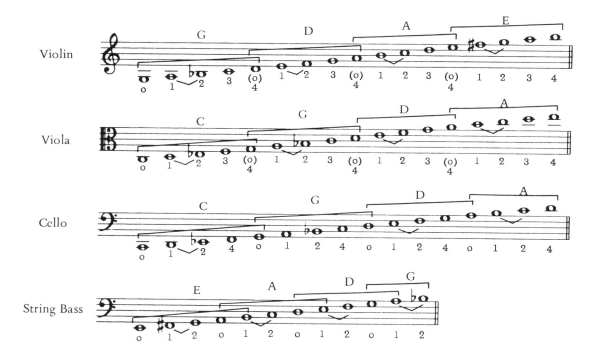

1. Keep your bow on the string during the rests and try to hear the pitch of each successive note before placing the fingers down.
2. Repeat Exercise 2–4 and 2–5 on the remaining strings.

*Cello: When using fourth finger, be sure to set down the third finger—even though it is not used in this pattern.

EXERCISE 2–4

EXERCISE 2–5

EXERCISE 2–6

Practice points:
- Drop and lift the fingers in an elastic manner.
- Hear and "feel" the distance of a whole- or half-step.

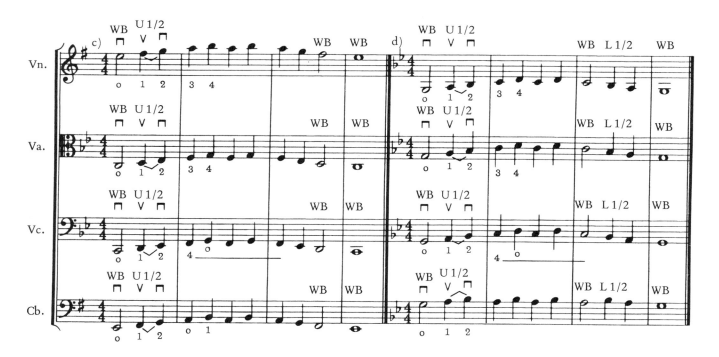

Practice points:
- Keep the left thumb in its correct relation to the fingers.
- Keep the left shoulder in its normal, relaxed position.

CHORALE: *ZEUCH EIN ZU DEINEN THOREN*

J. S. Bach

Finger Pattern III

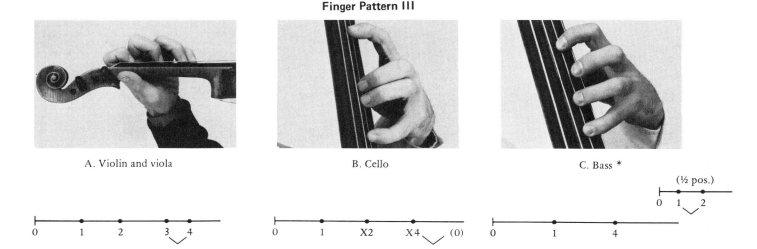

A. Violin and viola   B. Cello   C. Bass *

The pitches created by Finger Pattern III are identical in sound to the first five notes in a *Lydian* scale on the sequence *fa-sol-la-ti-do.*

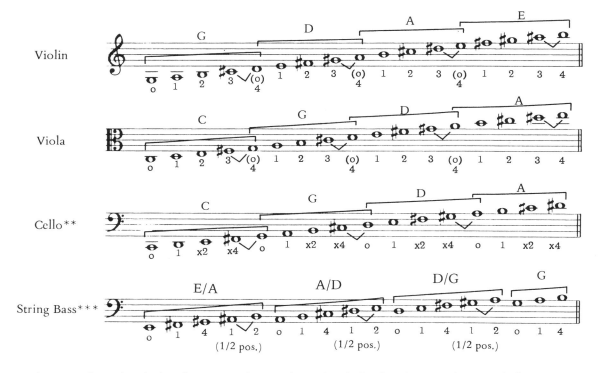

1. Keep you bow on the string during the rests and try to hear the pitch of each successive note before placing the fingers down.
2. Repeat Exercises 2–7 and 2–8 on the remaining strings.

*See illustration C., p. 56.

**Cello: In the normal or *closed hand position,* the span between the first and fourth fingers covers the interval of a minor third. To produce the pitches in Finger Pattern III, the second and fourth fingers are extended forward by one half-step—thus increasing the interval span to a major third. This expansion of the hand is variously called the *forward extension* or *open hand position.* To execute this, the thumb moves forward with the second finger and remains under it. Care must be taken that the first finger is not pulled off normal position during this motion. The indication for a forward extension or open hand position is an "x" preceding a finger number: x2 and x4.

***String Bass: To complete the last two notes of Finger Pattern III, the hand must move from the first to half position (½). To position the hand for half position, the entire *hand and arm move back as a unit*—one half-step.

EXERCISE 2–7

EXERCISE 2–8

53

EXERCISE 2–9

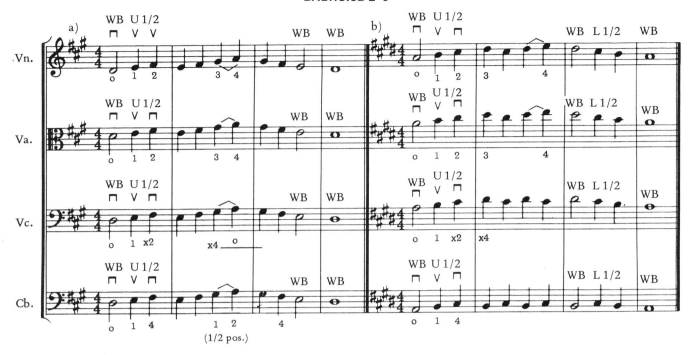

Practice points:
- Cello: Keep first finger anchored during the forward extension of the thumb and second finger.
- Keep fingers arched over the fingerboard.

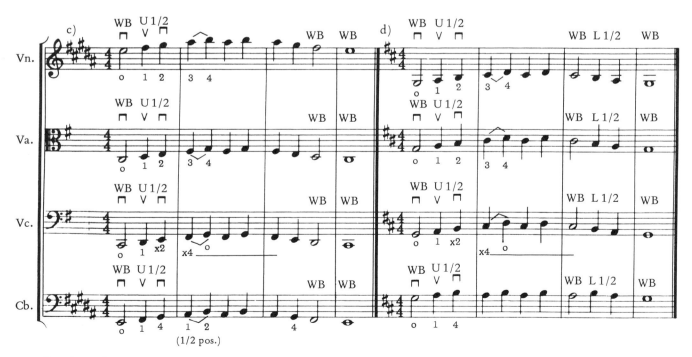

Practice points:
- Violin and viola: Keep "edge" of hand inclined toward the fingerboard when using the fourth finger.
- Keep fingertip centered on string.

THE BEAU STRATAGEM

English Folk Song

*Violin and Viola: Set Finger Pattern III silently on the D string before beginning. Verify the correctness of intonation of the fourth finger by testing its pitch against the sound of the open A string.

Finger Pattern IV

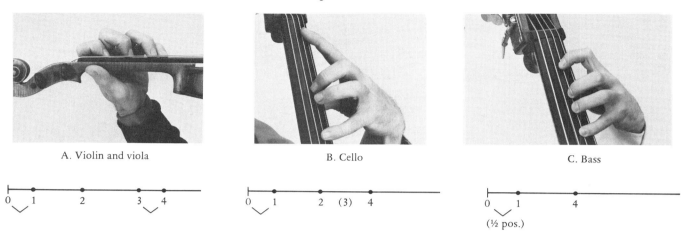

A. Violin and viola   B. Cello   C. Bass

The pitches created by Finger Pattern IV are identical in sound to the first five notes in a *Locrian* scale or the sequence *ti-do-re-mi-fa*.

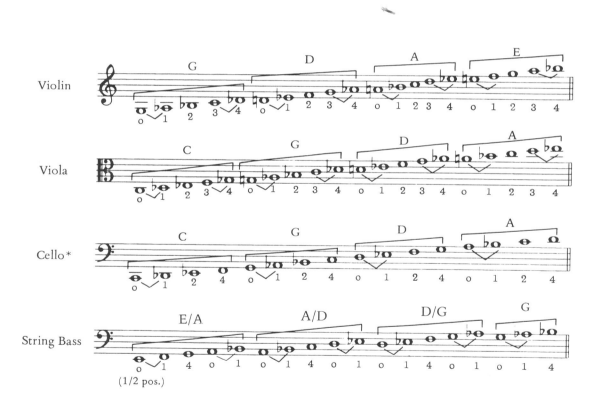

1. Keep your bow on the string during the rests and try to hear the pitch of each successive note before placing the fingers down.
2. Repeat Exercises 2–10 and 2–11 on the remaining strings.

*Cello: The half-step between the open string and first finger is achieved by another form of the *open hand position*: the *backward extension*. Again, the interval spanned between the first and fourth fingers is a major third. In this type of extension, the thumb *remains under* the second finger, while the first finger is extended backward one half-step. There is no special indication for the backward extension.

56

EXERCISE 2–10

EXERCISE 2–11

EXERCISE 2–12

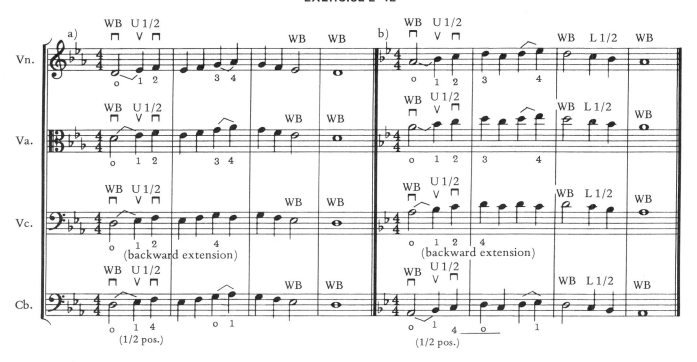

Practice points:

- Cello: Keep second and fourth fingers anchored during the backward extension.
- Violin and viola: Keep thumb in its usual position while placing the low first finger.

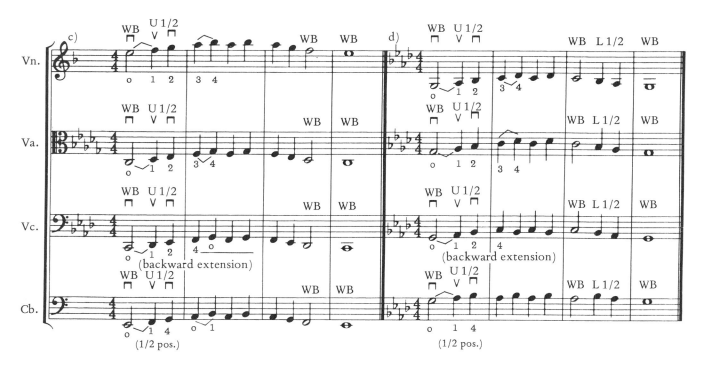

Practice points:

- Cello and Bass: Keep thumb under second finger.
- Violin and Viola: "Reach" up to third and fourth fingers whenever low first finger is used.

MELODY IN THE LOCRIAN MODE

Oddo

* ⤴ Lift and reset the bow on the string in a circular, counter-clockwise motion.

Mixed Finger Patterns

EXERCISE 2–13

1. Keep your bow on the string during the rests and try to hear the pitch of each successive note before placing the fingers down.
2. Repeat Exercises 2–13, 2–14, and 2–15 on the remaining strings.

EXERCISE 2–14

EXERCISE 2–15

Changing Finger Patterns

Repeat Exercises 2–16 through 2–20 on the remaining strings.

EXERCISE 2–16

EXERCISE 2–17

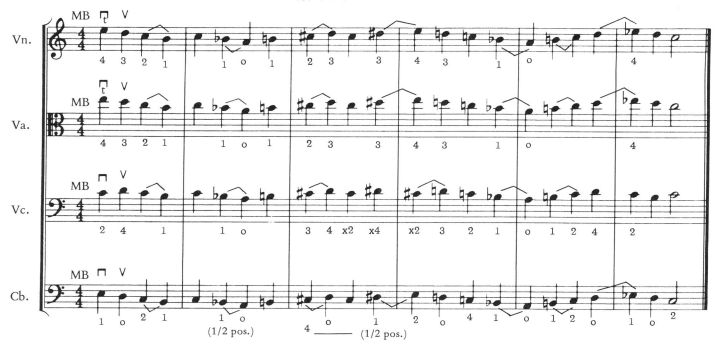

EXERCISE 2–18

EXERCISE 2–19

EXERCISE 2–20

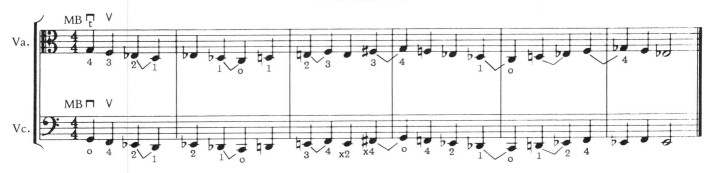

OLD GERMAN ROUND: *DIE MUSICI*

Moderato

Anonymous

64

SECTION II

In the previous exercises of this chapter, we were concerned with the development of the basic finger patterns, using a separate bow stroke for each note. When a slur (⌢) connects two or more notes, they are played with the bow moving continuously without changing direction. In this section we will further develop the finger patterns, while including basic slurred bowings as well.

The exercises in this section are divided into three units, with each unit emphasizing one of the most common types of slurred bowings:

Unit I: slurring 2 notes in one bow
Unit II: slurring 3 notes in one bow
Unit III: slurring 4 notes in one bow

Bow Distribution

To establish the correct concept of slurred bowings, the note values in a slurred figure should be played with a *proportionate* distribution of the bow. In the early stages, the notes should be played with as long a bow as possible—dividing the bow in halves for two-note slurs; thirds for three-note slurs; and quarters for four-note slurs. In more advanced applications of the slur, the relationship between note values and bow distribution may not be as exact.

String Crossing

So long as the slurred notes are played on one string, and the relationship between note values and bow distribution is balanced, coordination between the left and right hands can be established without too much difficulty. When string crosses occur in the midst of a slur, however, two new problems can be encountered. At the moment of the string cross the student may a) increase the speed of the bow, and/or (b) overcompensate for the distance of the string cross causing the bow to lunge to the new string.

The problem of maintaining an even bow speed at the point of a string cross can be corrected by drawing the students' attention to proportionate bow distribution. To solve the second problem, encourage the students to anticipate the string cross and affect a "rolling" motion of the arm and bow into the new string.

Bow Imagery

When a melodic pattern contains pitches that can be bowed only on adjacent or successively different strings, the young student will often interpret the visual impression of the pattern literally—incorrectly transferring to the bow arm a motion that closely approximates the pattern's melodic contour.

Bow imagery is a means of assisting the students in translating the visual impression of a melodic pattern into the correct *physical* concept of the bow stroke. This is achieved by providing graphic models that illustrate the melodic con-

tour of the pattern, its literal (incorrect) transfer, and the correct bow image.

With rare exceptions, the movement of the bow through the down- and up-bow cycles is not angular, but follows a configuration that is kinetically and visually curved.* The curvature of the bow stroke between the down- and up-bow cycles permits a smooth connection of the strokes between the changes of bow direction. Application of this principle will also affect a smoother connection in *legato* playing between slurred notes across and between strings.

The relationships between melodic contour, literal transfer, and correct bow image are readily apparent when they are juxtaposed. For example, the visual impression of the following pattern is one of the distance between notes—a disjunct melodic contour:

The physiological response to this impression results in a bow motion that is almost an exact duplication of the angularity of the pitch distances. Because the transfer is literal, the bow will lunge from pitch to pitch, and string to string.

If the high and low notes of the pattern are connected so that the angles are smoothed into a curve—somewhat like averaging the distances between the notes—the correct bow image is revealed.

The wavelike image suggests the kinetic sensation to be developed in the bow arm. The curvature of the image also indicates how to perform this pattern properly. Its shape reveals that the bow "leans" in the direction of the second note or string while still playing the first.

Bearing in mind that the correct bow motion is essentially curved motion, bow images are readily extracted for most patterns. Since most bowing problems are encountered when moving between strings, a variety of string-crossing patterns, literal transfers, and bow images is provided in Table 2–1.

*This should not be confused with the angle of the bow to the string—where the kinetic concept is to draw the bow in a *straight line.*

TABLE 2-1.

Pitch Pattern*	Literal Transfer (Incorrect)	Bow Image: Correct	
		Violin/Viola	Cello/Bass**

Unit I: Slurring Two Notes in One Bow

At this point it will be helpful to review the basic principles of "Bow Motion" and the "Use of the Whole Bow"— Chapter 1, p. 28-29.

EXERCISE 2–21

Notes for Table 2–1

*For the sake of simplicity, only strings of the violin are used in illustration. However, transfers and images remain the same for all instruments when the bow moves between adjacent and successive strings.

**Because cello and bass view the bridge from the fingerboard side and the violin and viola view the bridge from the tailpiece side, the images will be opposite.

†The transfers are shown for the violin and viola only. The same figure for the cello and bass would be upside-down.

‡Shapes are approximate. Properly performed, the bow plane would be narrower.

§The broken lines at the end of some figures indicate the continuation of the stroke into the next cycle.

#The lines intersecting the curves show the beginning and approximate locations of successive pitches in the pattern.

Note: As the tempo increases for each pattern the shape of the image remains essentially the same—but somewhat contracted. When bowing patterns are reversed (beginning up-bow instead of down-bow) the image will be a mirror reverse of the curve indicated.

EXERCISE 2–22 *

EXERCISE 2–23

*See *Bow Image* 7, p. 66.

** ↗ Lift and reset the bow at the frog for the next measure.

EXERCISE 2-24

MELODY IN A

Mozart

Unit II: Slurring Three Notes in One Bow

EXERCISE 2–25

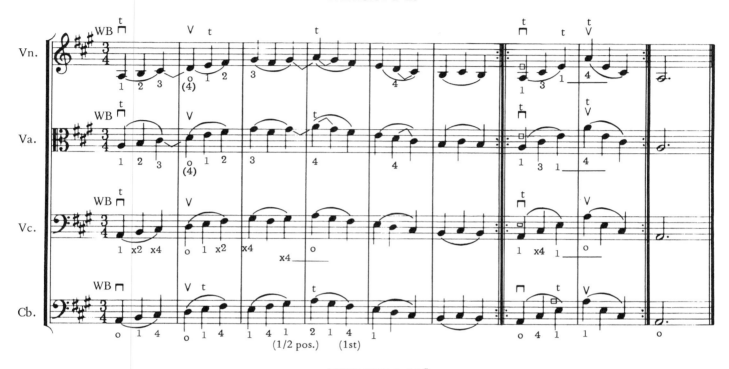

EXERCISE 2–26 *

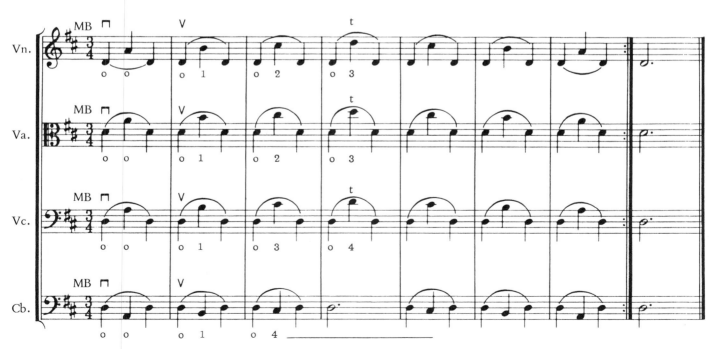

*See *Bow Image* 1, p. 66.

EXERCISE 2–27

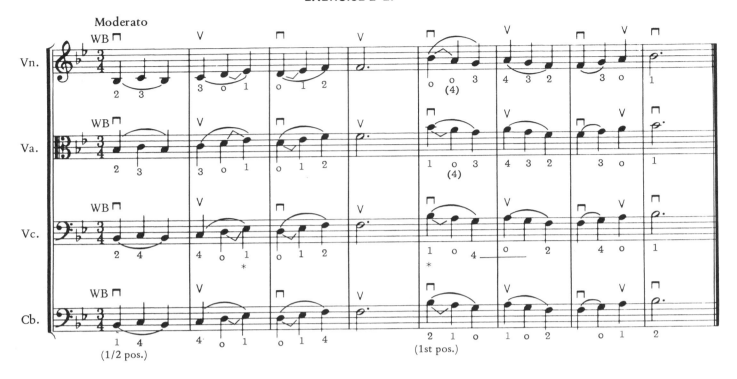

EXERCISE 2–28

*Backward extension.

MELODY

Grazioso

Mendelssohn

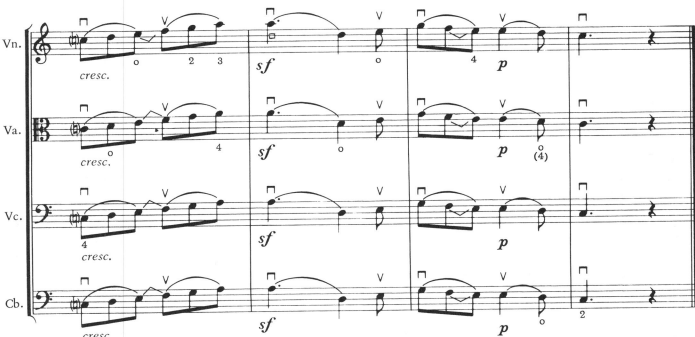

Unit III: Slurring Four Notes in One Bow

EXERCISE 2–29

EXERCISE 2–30*

*See *Bow Image* 6, p. 66.

EXERCISE 2–31

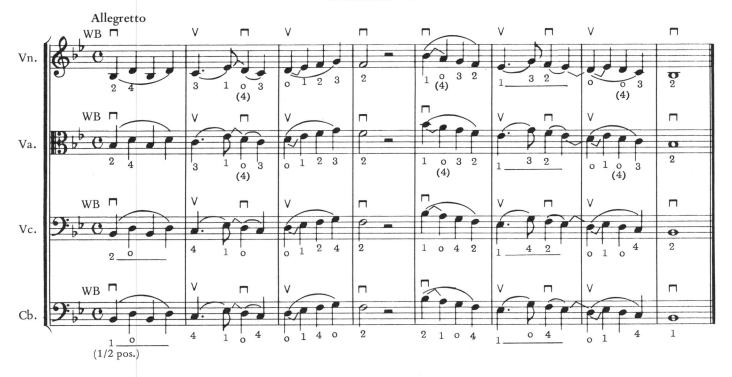

EXERCISE 2–32

BAGATELLE

Schumann

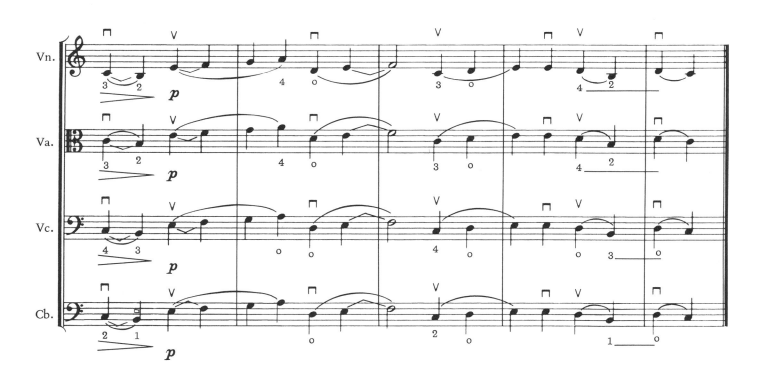

DUET NO. 18 FROM *DIDO AND AENEAS*

Purcell
arr. Oddo

Finger Exercises*

The following exercises are useful for the development of finger dexterity, intonation, and bow-finger coordination. Each exercise consists of four notes in a variety of finger patterns. Depending on the string chosen, and whether the pattern begins with the hand set a whole- or half-step above the open string, each exercise will produce a differenct series of pitches. If, for example, the finger pattern 1 2 3 ⌣ 4 is played on the D string—for the violin or viola—the resultant pitches may be either E   F# G# ⌣ A or E♭   F   G ⌣ A♭.

Practice procedures. Throughout all finger exercises, remember to verify the intonation of those pitches that share the same letter-name as one of the open strings. As you practice, start slowly at first, then increase the difficulty through the following means:

1. Play all nine finger patterns *consecutively*.
2. Play one finger pattern with nine *consecutive* bowing variations.
3. Play the nine finger patterns—each with a *different* bowing variation.
4. Gradually increase the speed of performance.

Finger Exercises

Violin/Viola

a)	1 ⌣ 2	3	4		d)	3 ⌣ 2	1	4		g)	2 ⌣ 1	3	4
b)	1	3 ⌣ 2	4		e)	3	1 ⌣ 2	4		h)	2	3 ⌣ 4	1
c)	1	4 ⌣ 3	2		f)	3 ⌣ 4	2	1		i)	2 ⌣ 3	1	4

Cello

a)	0	1	3 ⌣ 4		d)	1	0	3 ⌣ 4		g)	2 ⌣ 1	3 ⌣ 4	
b)	0	2 ⌣ 1	4		e)	1 ⌣ 2	4	3		h)	2 ⌣ 3	1	4
c)	0	1	x2	4		f)	1 ⌣ 2 ⌣ 3 ⌣ 4			i)	0 ⌣ 1	2	4

String Bass

a)	0	1	4	1		d)	1	0	2 ⌣ 1		g)	2	4	1 ⌣ 2	
b)	0	1 ⌣ 2	1		e)	2 ⌣ 1	4	1		h)	1	4	2	4
c)	0	4	1 ⌣ 2		f)	1 ⌣ 2	4	1		i)	2	4	0	1

Bowing Variations

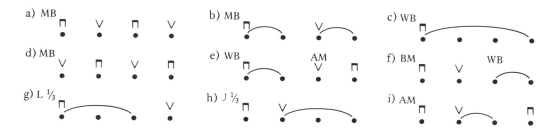

---

*To be used for individual practice.

Chapter 3

ETUDES AND BOWING PATTERNS
FOR INDIVIDUAL INSTRUMENTS

The previous studies provided a foundation for basic right- and left-hand techniques. Those techniques will now be extended and integrated through the practice of three etudes (with bowing patterns) specifically designed for *individual instruments*. The coordination between the left hand and single and slurred bowings will be developed within the framework of three categories of etudes:

Etude No. 1: Scale lines
Etude No. 2: Arpeggios
Etude No. 3: String crossings

Practicing the Etudes

Practice each etude as printed, starting slowly to familiarize yourself with the fingerings and string crosses. At first, you may wish to start pizzicato, adding the bow later. As you gain facility, tempo should be increased. When the problems of the left hand have been mastered, proceed to the bowing patterns.

Practicing the Bowing Patterns

The bowing patterns accompanying each etude are arranged in increasing order of difficulty. As with the etude, start your practice of a bowing pattern slowly, increasing the tempo as facility is acquired. Experiment with each pattern by playing it in different tempos. When whole-bow (WB) is indicated you may find that it is impractical to play the pattern at faster tempos, and middle-bow (MB) playing should be substituted.

The first measure of all patterns should begin with the down-bow. But because of the location of the slurs, alternate measures may begin with the bow moving in the reverse direction. In such patterns, the portion of the bow used will also be reversed:

For nonreversing patterns, the cycle of down-bow beginnings will repeat automatically.

For all bowing patterns it would be helpful to review *Bow Imagery*, pp. 65-66.

ETUDES AND BOWING PATTERNS FOR VIOLIN

ETUDE NO. 1

BOWING PATTERNS FOR ETUDE NO. 1

ETUDE NO. 2

(Violin)

BOWING PATTERNS FOR ETUDE NO. 2

ETUDE NO. 3

BOWING PATTERNS FOR ETUDE NO. 3

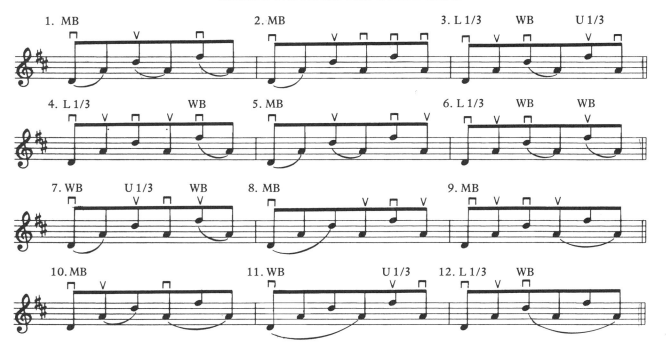

ETUDES AND BOWING PATTERNS FOR VIOLA

ETUDE NO. 1

BOWING PATTERNS FOR ETUDE NO. 1

ETUDE NO. 2

BOWING PATTERNS FOR ETUDE NO. 2

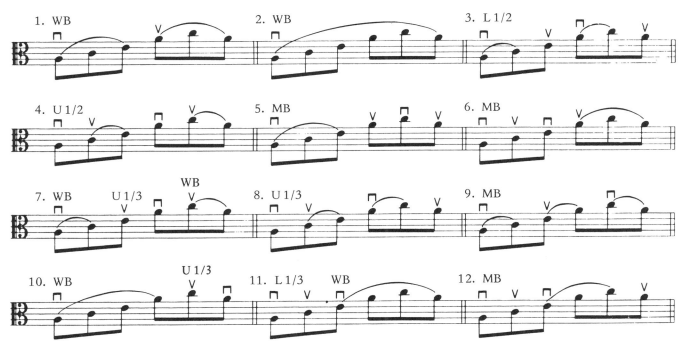

84

ETUDE NO. 3

BOWING PATTERNS FOR ETUDE NO. 3

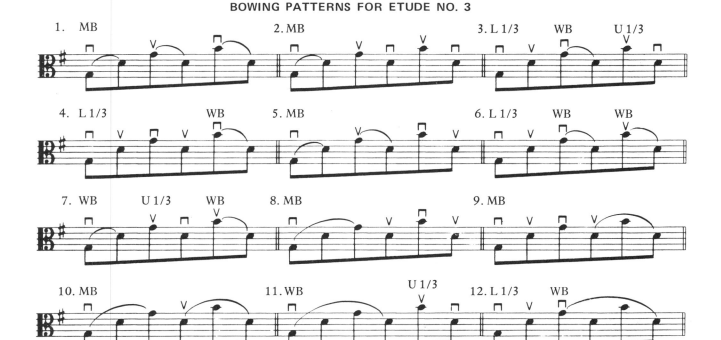

ETUDES AND BOWING PATTERNS FOR CELLO

ETUDE NO. 1

BOWING PATTERNS FOR ETUDE NO. 1

ETUDE NO. 2

BOWING PATTERNS FOR ETUDE NO. 2

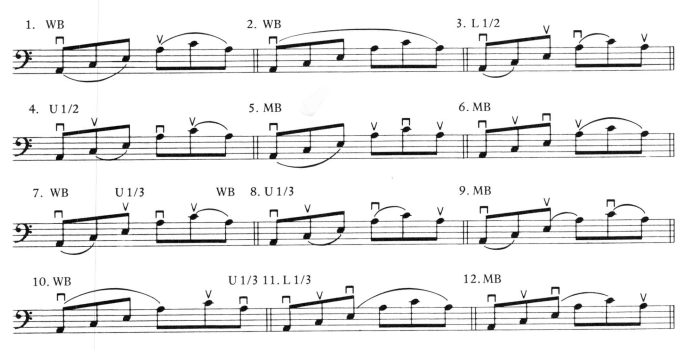

ETUDE NO. 3

BOWING PATTERNS FOR ETUDE NO. 3

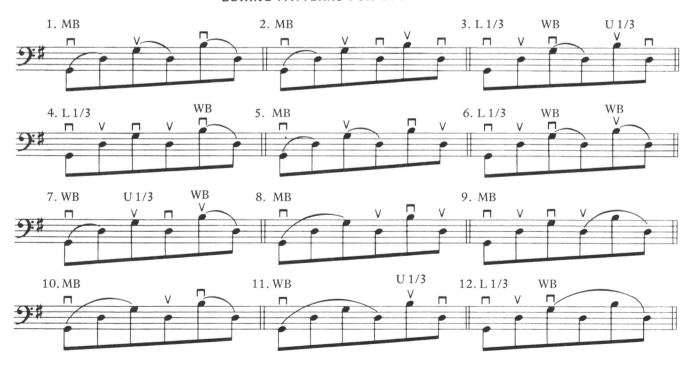

ETUDES AND BOWING PATTERNS FOR STRING BASS

ETUDE NO. 1

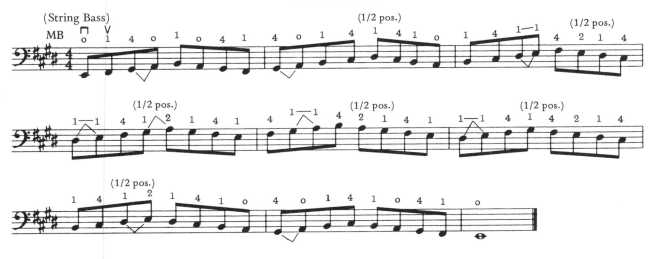

BOWING PATTERNS FOR ETUDE NO. 1

ETUDE NO. 2

(String Bass)

BOWING PATTERNS FOR ETUDE NO. 2

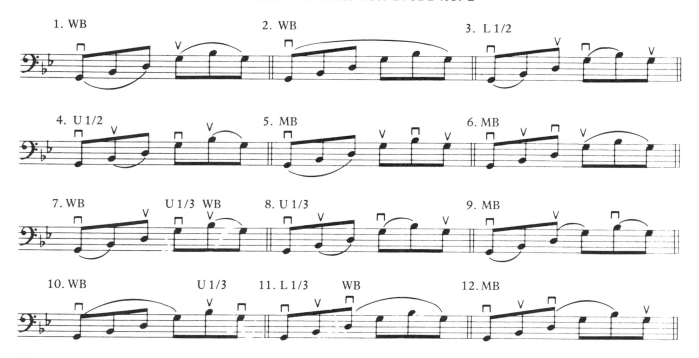

ETUDE NO. 3

BOWING PATTERNS FOR ETUDE NO. 3

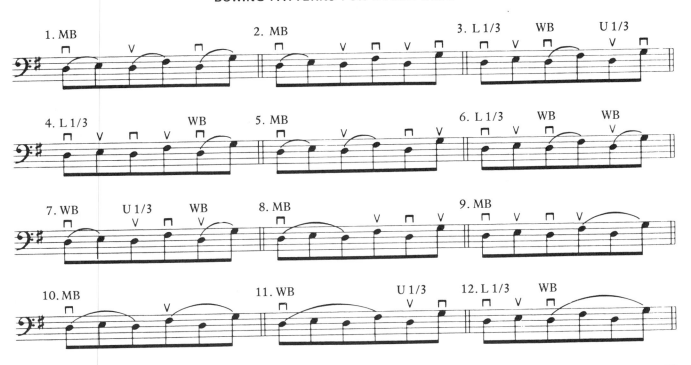

Chapter 4

CHAMBER MUSIC SELECTIONS

The chamber music selections in this chapter provide the opportunity to review and integrate the techniques studied so far: basic bowing, finger patterns, the détaché stroke, and slurring of two and three notes in one bow.

The performance of these selections need not be limited to large ensembles only. For variety, they may be played with one player on each part—as a quintet of two violins, viola, cello, and bass, for example. While the quintet is performing, the remainder of the class will observe the performance, then provide a critique suggesting corrections of posture, holding the instrument and bow, tone production, bow distribution, etc.

AMERICA
(My Country 'Tis of Thee)

*The bowing figures of 𝅘𝅥. 𝅘𝅥𝅮 and 𝅘𝅥 𝅘𝅥 are executed by dividing the bow proportionately (by note value) and making a slight pause between each note—without changing bow direction.

94

Grieg
arr. Oddo

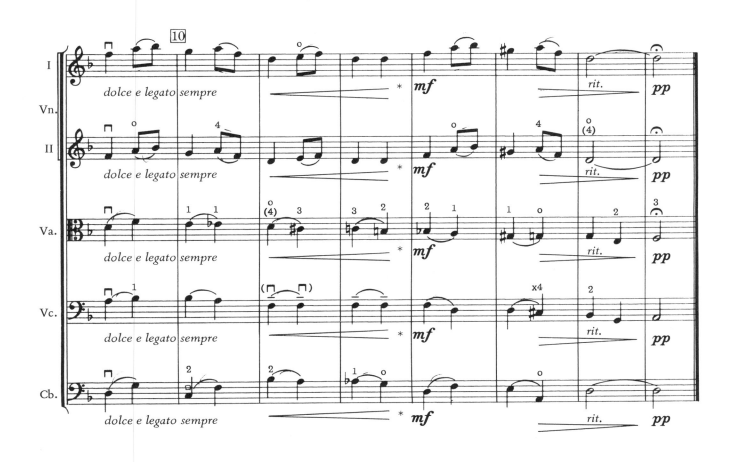

*The *crescendo* (————) and *diminuendo* (————) are executed by controlling increases or de-creases in the weight and/or speed of the bow. In measures 11 and 12, bow speed and weight are gradually increased until measure 13, where the dynamic level of *mf* is reached. Beginning at the end of measure 14 and continuing to the end of the piece, bow speed and weight are gradually decreased until the dynamic level of *pp* is reached in the last measure.

EXCERPT FROM *CONCERTO IN D MAJOR*

Vivaldi

Notes for p. 99

*Play both top and bottom notes simultaneously.
**See Chapter 5, "Positions and Principles of Shifting."

EXCERPT FROM *SYMPHONY NO. 4*, THIRD MOVEMENT

Tchaikovsky

FUGUE FROM *ARIADNE MUSICA* (NO. 10)

J. K. F. Fischer
arr. Oddo

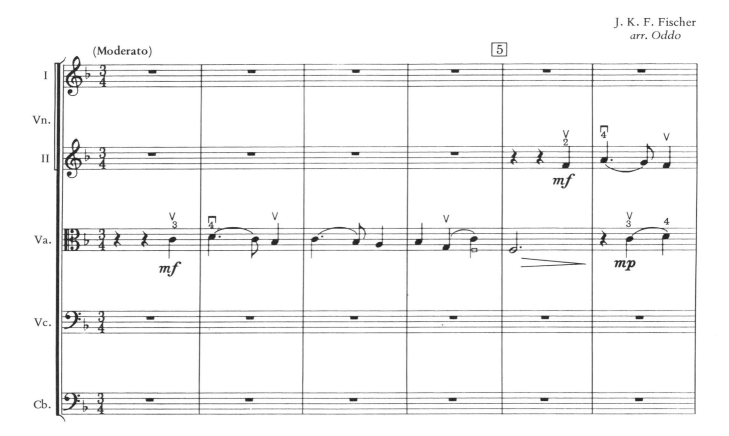

100

Chapter 5

INTERMEDIATE CONCEPTS
OF STRING PLAYING AND TEACHING

POSITIONS AND PRINCIPLES OF SHIFTING

We have often observed that advanced string players rarely play an entire composition with the left hand remaining fixed at the scroll end of the fingerboard. It is more characteristic to see the hand's position shifted frequently along different lengths of the string.

The distance spanned by the first and fourth fingers of the left hand vary from instrument to instrument. Violinists and violists, for example, can span the interval of a fourth. But because of the longer string lengths on the larger instruments, cellists can span only a third, while bassists cover just a whole-step between the first and fourth fingers. Because of the limited span, cellists and bassists are introduced to the principles of shifting and position work at a comparatively earlier stage than are violinists or violists. Without this, the lower instruments would be limited to only the most rudimentary studies. Even fairly simple passages would be awkward if not impossible without basic shifting and position work.

While the main function of the shift and position changing is to extend the range of the instrument, this technique offers other advantages:

1. Eliminates awkward string crossing and fingerings.
2. Maintains the sonority or color of a single string.
3. Facilitates large interval leaps.
4. Avoids unnecessary use of open strings.

Identifying the Positions

The types of symbols used to identify the positions are not applied consistently in all string publications. An examination of class materials in strings, especially for cello and string bass, will reveal that some have a different numerical basis for labeling the positions. Some writers prefer to use roman numerals; others use arabic numerals. Either numeral may be further qualified by indications for intermediate and half positions.

Editors and some composers may indicate fingerings, but rarely the position to be used; this is the responsibility of the performer. However, they will often designate that a certain passage is to be played on a given string by placing a roman numeral with dashes above that passage. IV——, for example, indicates that the passage must be played on the fourth or *lowest* string only. Because of a possible confusion between the two interpretations of roman numerals— one for labeling positions, the other for indicating a string— this text will use arabic numerals (1st, 3rd, etc.) to designate positions.

Determining the Position

The numbering of a position is determined by two factors: the location of the index finger in relation to the open string; and the interval or degree-name of that note. Generally, if the index finger is a whole-step above an open string, it is *1st position*; two steps above, *2nd position*; three steps, *3rd position,* etc. Exercise 5–1 illustrates these two factors.

EXERCISE 5-1

Exercise 5–1 is used here primarily for the explanation and illustration of *position numbering*, and should not be practiced as a playing exercise until the completion of Exercise 5–4.

Sul D—to be played entirely on the D string.

Shifting and higher position work may be introduced as soon as students can demonstrate a command of basic finger patterns, coordination of bow and finger movement, and the establishment of the proper shape or set of the left hand and arm. To achieve a smooth and accurate change of position and shift, the following principles must be observed:

1. The shift is executed by slightly releasing the pressure of the left thumb and fingers, moving the hand lightly to the next position. But care must be taken to prevent a stabbing or jerking movement.

2. Generally, the shift occurs *on the beat,* but its speed is always determined by the musical context: fast passsages require quick shifts; slower passages, more expressive shifts.

3. Encourage students to sing or hear the pitch of the "target" note of the shift *before* the shift. Whenever possible, the pitch of the new note should be compared to the pitch of an open string to test the accuracy of the shift.

4. The basic motion of the shift requires that the left hand and arm move as a basic unit or bloc, moving to the new position without a change in the basic shape of either.

5. The left elbow, hand, thumb, and fingers must be relaxed and loose during the shift.

6. At the point of the shift, the finger that is on the string *remains on the string* until the hand arrives at the new position. After the new position has been reached, the remaining fingers complete the finger pattern.

7. The spacing between the fingers decreases in distance for each successively higher position.

In addition to the application of these seven principles, accurate shifting requires the development of aural-tactile skills. The relationship between these two skills is important because each acts as "feedback" for the other. Both skills are integrated into a unified technique by first hearing the pitch of the target note, then comparing it with the sensation in the thumb and shifting finger as they measure the distance the hand must travel to arrive at the target note and position.

EXERCISE 5—2. SHIFTING WITH THE SAME FINGER

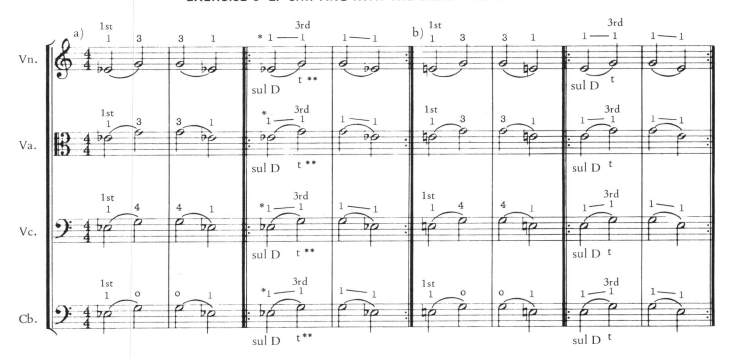

*Shift directly to the new position, keeping the first finger down.
**A note with a "t" may be tested for accuracy by comparing it to an open string of the same letter name.

Practice Exercise 5-2 in the following ways:
1. Transpose and play on remaining strings.
2. Play in the following rhythms:

EXERCISE 5-3. SHIFTING FROM AN OPEN STRING*

In this exercise, the thumb is the guide. Keep its pressure light enough to permit the hand, wrist, and arm to move as a single unit. Do not let thumb lag behind.

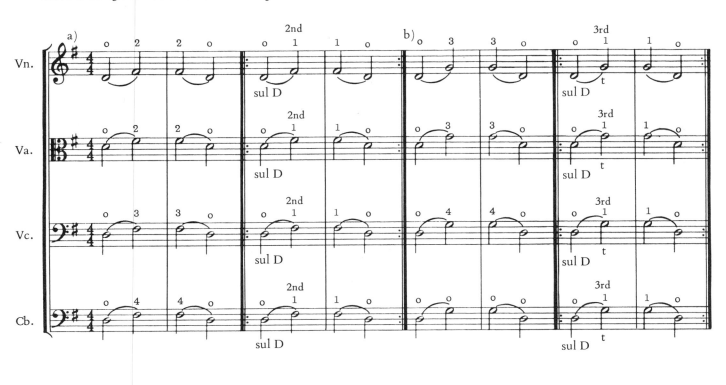

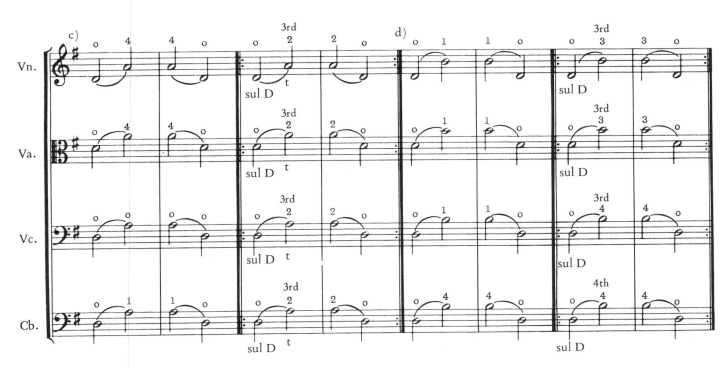

*For supplemental exercises, see end of Exercise 5–2.

Shifting with Different Fingers

When shifting with different fingers, the finger that is on the string remains on the string until the shift is completed with the new finger. The finger that remains on the string during the shift is called the *guide finger* and serves to link the original position to the new position.

In early shifting studies, the guide finger is indicated by the grace-note symbol placed between the main notes: ♩♪♩ . At first, this type of shift should be practiced slowly so that the slide up to the guide finger is audible. Later, as facility is acquired, the sound of the slide should be eliminated. In different-finger shifting, the second note must occur on the beat, with the time needed for the shift being derived from a fraction of the first note.

EXERCISE 5–4. SHIFTING WITH DIFFERENT FINGERS*

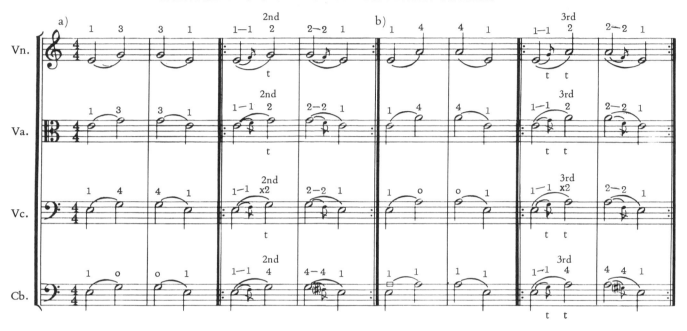

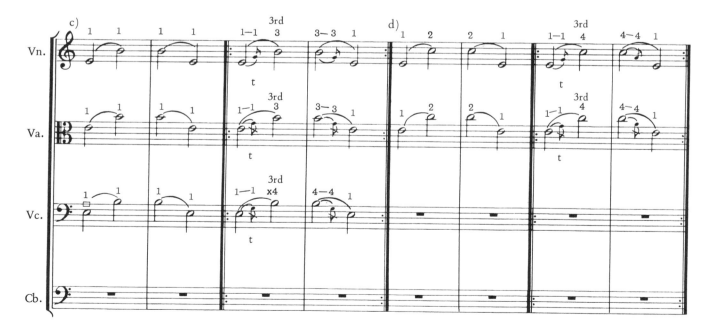

Return to Exercise 5–1, playing it first with single bows, then slurring three notes in a bow.

*For supplemental exercises, see end of Exercise 5–2.

BOWING TECHNIQUES, SCALES, AND ARPEGGIOS

The techniques illustrated in this section represent some of the most common orchestral and solo bowings. Each bowing is presented in the framework of a major scale and arpeggio.* Before attempting to master each bowing technique, practice its scale and arpeggio pattern several times in the manner shown below.

This practice will allow you to familiarize yourself with the finger patterns, string crosses, shifts, and positions.

Scales

Arpeggios

1. pizz.
2. arco

*Minor scales and arpeggios begin on p. 117.

Martelé

Martelé is a sharply accented or "hammered" stroke with a clean separation between notes. The bowing is performed in the middle to upper part of the bow with separate down-up strokes. At the start of each stroke, press the bow into the string with a slight rotation of the forearm and hand; pull the bow quickly and release the pressure at the same time. The motion must end with a clean stop before changing bow direction. Martelé may be indicated by the symbols ʌ or > or • placed above each note, by a dynamic marking (*sf*), or by the word *marcato* over the passage.

EXERCISE 5–5. MARTELÉ

*Alternate fingerings are in parentheses.

Hooked Bowing

Hooked bowing involves the connection of two notes of *unequal* value in the same bow direction—with a slight pause between each. The bowing may be performed in any part of the bow. It is used mainly to avoid awkward bowings or incorrectly placed accents. Hooked bowing is indicated by a slur with an articulation mark, either a dot or a dash: a) or b) etc. The bow is divided proportionately by note value. In a), for example, the quarter note is played with two-thirds of the bow and the eighth note with the remaining third.

EXERCISE 5–6. HOOKED BOWING

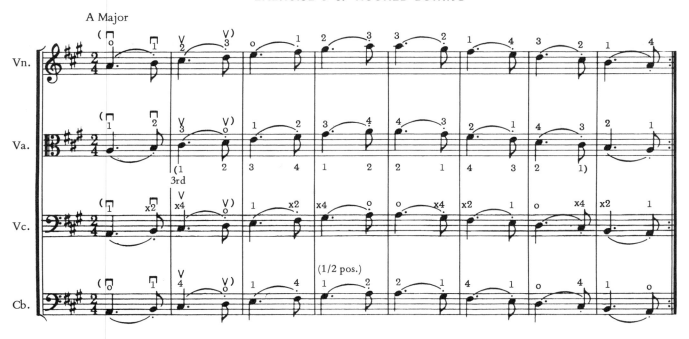

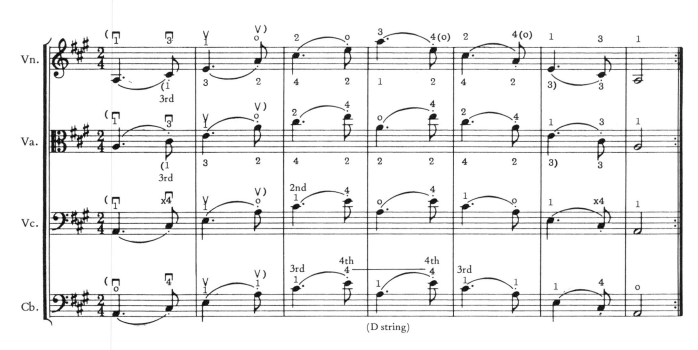

Louré or Portato

The louré or portato is a bowing style in which each note in a series of slurred notes is given a distinct pulse—without a pause between each note. The bowing may be performed at any part of the bow, but is generally a mid-bow stroke. The pulses are dynamic in origin and are created by the slight addition—then subtraction—of bow weight at the beginning of each note. This is achieved by a slight increase—then decrease—of first-finger pressure. A slur and dashes above or below a series of notes is the usual indication for louré bowing.

EXERCISE 5–7. LOURÉ (OR PORTATO)

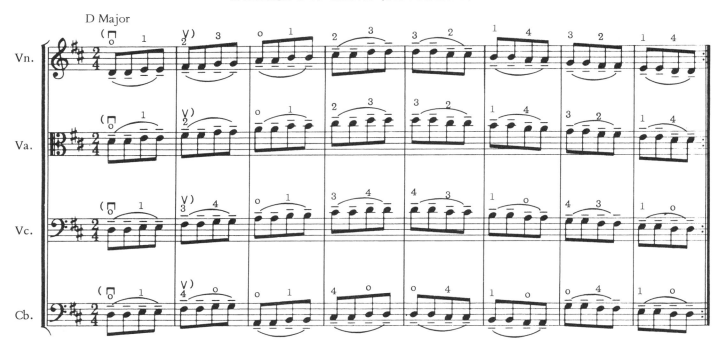

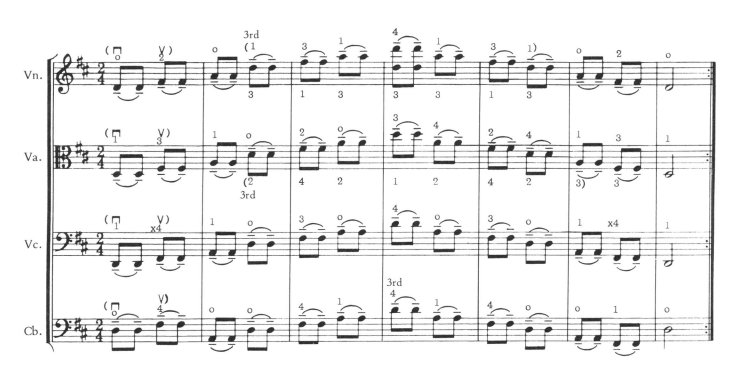

Slurred Staccato

As the name implies, this stroke involves a series of short notes played in one bow direction, with a slight pause between each note. The bowing is actually a series of successive martelé-like strokes which are controlled by the rotation of the forearm and hand. While the stroke can be executed in either bow direction, it is most successfully performed up-bow, from the tip to the middle of the bow. Slurred staccato is indicated by a series of notes with *dots* connected by a slur:  , etc.

EXERCISE 5–8. SLURRED STACCATO

113

Spiccato

Spiccato bowing is a springing or bouncing stroke that is executed below the middle of the bow. The precise part of the bow is governed by the speed and dynamics of the passage. The stroke is initiated in the forearm in a down-up brushing motion, about an inch above the string. To get the correct motion, drop the bow against the string in a swinging movement (⌣) using the natural spring of the bow. With the hand and fingers very relaxed, this brushing motion will cause the bow to bounce. In the spicatto stroke the hair of the bow should strike the string a bit closer to the fingerboard, where the string is more resilient.

EXERCISE 5–9. SPICCATO

Ricochet or Jeté

In ricochet or jeté bowing, the motion is identical with the spiccato (bouncing) stroke except that the bow is allowed to bounce two or more times before the direction is changed. Ricochet is always executed down-bow, and usually from the middle to upper part of the bow. The stroke is performed by keeping the wrist and fingers loose, dropping the bow on the string (mid-bow) while moving it down-bow. The indication for ricochet is a series of notes with dots, connected by a slur that begins with the down-bow: , for example.

EXERCISE 5–10. RICOCHET (OR JETÉ)

Tremolo

The *tremolo* is an orchestral bowing calling for the most rapid alternation of short up and down strokes as is possible. The stroke is performed in the upper third of the bow with a rather rigid arm for loud dynamics; at the tip of the bow with a flexible wrist for very soft passages. Tremolos may be accented by starting with a fast stroke from the middle of the bow to the tip, followed by rapid short strokes. Starting the stroke at the tip of the bow and moving toward the middle will produce a crescendo, while the reverse procedure produces a diminuendo. The tremolo is indicated by short, incomplete beams on a note stem: ♩ or ♩ .

EXERCISE 5–11. TREMOLO

Minor Scales—Chromatic Scale—Whole-Tone Scale

Below each of the following exercises for the minor scales and arpeggios, and the concluding chromatic and whole-tone scales, a set of optional bowing patterns is provided for additional practice.

EXERCISE 5–12

EXERCISE 5-13

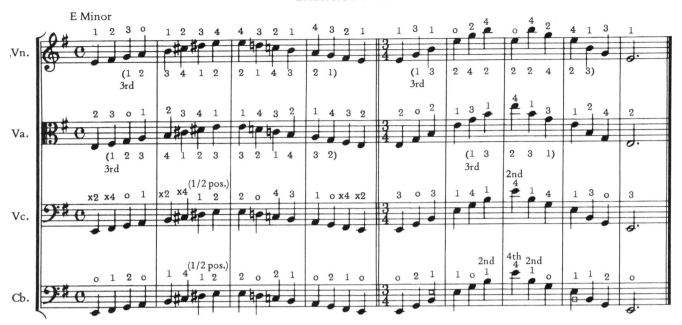

EXERCISE 5-14

118

EXERCISE 5-15

EXERCISE 5-16

EXERCISE 5–17

EXERCISE 5–18

*Touch string lightly—not against fingerboard—at a point halfway between bridge and fingerboard nut (see "Harmonics," pp. 129-130).

*Alternate fingerings are in parentheses.

Whole-Tone Scale

At the completion of this section, students may progress to Chapter 6, "Intermediate Chamber Music Selections."

DOUBLE STOPS, CHORDS, AND ARPEGGIOS

Double Stops

When two notes are sounded simultaneously, they are called *double stops*, a technique now somewhat familiar from the tuning procedures of Chapter 1. In symphonic and string orchestra literature, double stops may be written for two open strings, but more usually for one open string and one stopped (fingered) string. Double stops with two fingers on adjacent strings, while not very difficult to perform, occur mainly in solo literature.

Extended double stop playing in ensemble music is not a very common occurrence. When two (or more) notes are written to be sounded together, *divisi* is usually indicated. The usual procedure for divisi is this: the player in the "outside" chair plays the top note; the player on the "inside" chair plays the bottom note. Divisi by stands or sections is another possibility for playing simultaneous notes, but at the discretion of the composer or conductor—not the player.

Besides its harmonic contribution to the string sonority, double stop playing has other important side benefits: improved intonation, bow control, and set of the left hand.

Strangely enough, the study of double stop playing must first begin with exercises for the bow arm. Up to now, the bow has been moving on a single-string plane. This means that the player will have to learn the "feel" of three new bowing planes—one for each pair of strings—in order to sustain the sound of two strings.

Sustaining a clear and balanced tone for the double stop is achieved by establishing the correct bowing plane between strings, determining the proper amount of bow weight, and drawing the bow perfectly perpendicular to the strings. The beginner, assuming that two notes require twice as much bow weight as a single note, will often overwhelm the strings by excessive bow weight. And when the bow plane is not aligned correctly, the player frequently loses the sound of one of the strings. A bow that is too tight will also cause problems in producing a resonant double stop.

The exercises presented in this section serve as an introduction to the three basic types of double stops: two open strings; one open, one stopped; and two stopped strings. The exercises are written primarily for the violin, viola, and cello. Because double stops (and chords) are rarely written for the string bass, especially in school-level compositions, only the most rudimentary exercises are provided. However, the string bass players should familiarize themselves with this technique.

EXERCISE 5–21

*Bass: double stops optional.

EXERCISE 5–22

EXERCISE 5–23

*Bass: double stops optional.

124

EXERCISE 5-24

EXERCISE 5-25

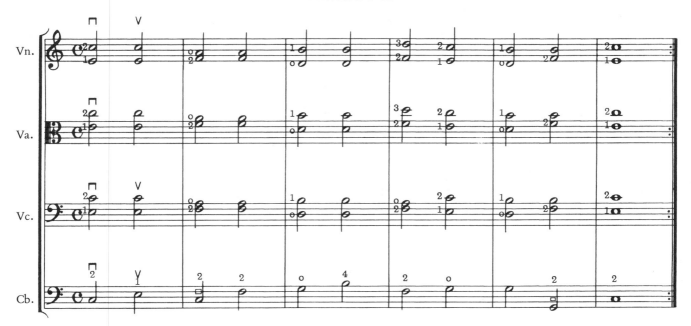

*Bass: bottom line and double stops optional.

Chords

Chords of three and four notes are effective for the violin, viola, and cello. In their notation, they are written as if they were to be sounded with a single attack, like a piano chord. In actual performance, this is rarely the case. Chords are written one way, but are performed in a variety of ways: broken chords, block chords, and divided chords.

In solo playing, three- and four-string chords are usually played as *broken chords*. In this type of chord, the lower two notes are sounded first, followed immediately by the upper two notes played as a double stop. While connecting the lower notes to the upper notes, the bow direction does not change. The chord is played in such a way that the bottom notes are like grace notes to the top notes. To produce a resonant sound in broken-chord playing, bow distribution is crucial. Only a relatively small portion of the bow must be used to play the bottom notes, with the remainder of the bow reserved for sustaining the full value of the top two notes. This type of bowing is most successfully executed down-bow.

EXERCISE 5–26. BROKEN CHORDS

The *block chord* of three strings—where all notes are sounded simultaneously—is a true triple stop and is performed as written. Its use is generally limited to solo writing. These chords, indicated by their shorter durations in a moderately fast tempo, are executed with successive down-bows using the full width of the bow hair. Furthermore, the chord is played in the lower part of the bow, close to the fingerboard—where the strings are more pliant—with the majority of the bow weight directed into the middle string.

126

EXERCISE 5–27. BLOCK CHORDS

As a general rule, all chords should be played with the bow on the string at the beginning of each stroke. In solo works—depending on the character, style period, etc., of the composition—chords may be played with the "bow in motion" approach. Here the bow is already moving above the strings before the chord is struck. The bow literally "lands" on the strings giving the chord a dramatic and explosive quality.

In ensemble music, three-note chords are usually per-formed divisi. In the divisi chord, the top two notes are played as a double stop by the "outside-stand" player; the bottom two notes by the "inside" player. The term *divisi* may appear over such passages, or the composer will specify the division of the chord by the manner in which the stems are connected to the note-heads. Since string crosses are no longer a problem, divisi chords may be played with alter-nating down- and up-bow strokes.

Arpeggios

Chords may be arpeggiated by playing each note individually without changing bow direction. When playing arpeggio chords, the bow "rolls" from string to string in a continuous and unbroken arclike movement. There should be no sensation of separate movements from note to note. The division of the bow must be balanced so that each chord member receives a proportionate amount of bow.

EXERCISE 5–28.   THREE-STRING ARPEGGIOS

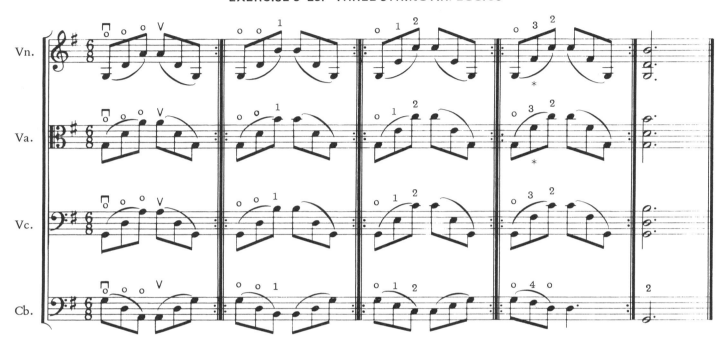

EXERCISE 5–29.   FOUR-STRING ARPEGGIOS

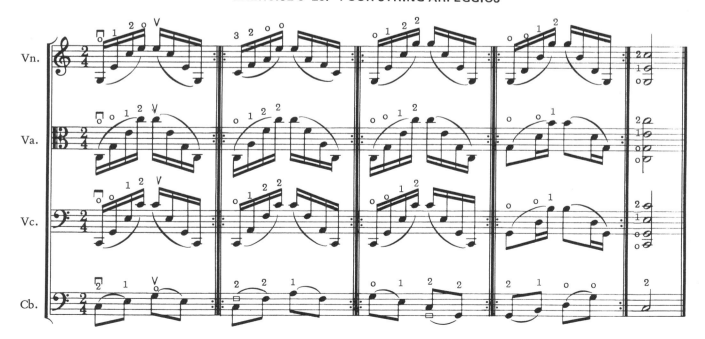

*A "cross fingering" is necessary here to produce the diminished fifth between the f# and c.

Finally, double stops and chords can be performed pizzicato, as well as with the bow. To achieve maximum resonance, this type of pizzicato is usually performed a bit farther away from the end of the fingerboard.

So that the notes will sound simultaneously, pizzicato double stops may be performed with the thumb or index finger. Chords are performed in a quick, sweeping motion (from bottom note to top note) across the strings, and at a slight angle to the fingerboard. The violinist and violist use the index finger, while the cellist uses the thumb. When executed correctly, individual strings will not be heard, only the sound of a full chord. (Return to some of the exercises for double stops and chords and play them pizzicato.)

HARMONICS: NATURAL AND ARTIFICIAL

The harmonic is a clear, flutelike sound that results when the string is touched lightly (but not against the fingerboard) at one of its natural dividing points or nodes. Placing the finger at a point that is a string division of 1/2, 1/4, 1/3, etc., permits the string to vibrate in segments rather than as a whole. That is, the overtone (harmonic) sounds rather than the fundamental (the stopped or open string).

The distinction between the two types of harmonics—*natural* and *artificial*—is a simple one. Natural harmonics are produced with only one finger lightly touching the string—usually the third or fourth. Artificial harmonics, however, are produced with two fingers: one stopping the string, the other touching the string lightly at one of its nodes—usually in first and fourth finger combinations. (See Figures 5-30 and 5-31.)

Natural harmonics are quite common in orchestral literature, and are easily produced on all string instruments. Artificial harmonics, while found in orchestral compositions, exist mainly in music of a solo nature and are most successfully produced on the violin and viola.

A small circle placed over a note and/or a diamond-shaped note-head are the usual symbols for the notation of a natural harmonic. However, the fingerings for the harmonic may not always be indicated. Artificial harmonics are notated with a regular note-head for the stopped note and a diamond-shaped note indicating where the finger touches the string lightly.

Because of the relatively shorter string segments, harmonics should be bowed a bit closer to the bridge and with less bow weight. In natural harmonics, only one finger must touch the string; all others must be lifted away from the string. In addition, if the placement of the finger is not absolutely exact, or its pressure too great, the harmonic will not sound—only a squeak or scratch.

The most common type is the octave or half-string natural harmonic. This harmonic sounds in the same register as written. All other harmonics, whether natural or artificial, sound higher than written. The written symbol, string division, and actual sound of some common harmonics are illustrated in Tables 5-1 and 5-2.

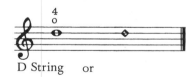

D String   or

Figure 5-30. Natural harmonics.

or

Figure 5-31. Artificial harmonics.

Table 5-1. Natural Harmonics.

*Concert pitch.

Table 5–2. Artificial Harmonics.*

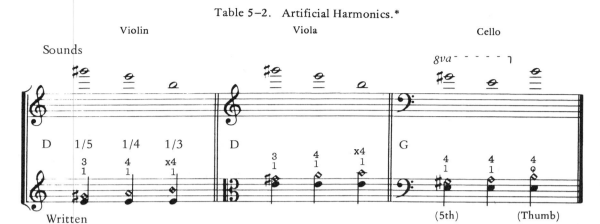

*Because of the limited span between the first and fourth fingers, artificial harmonics are generally impractical on the string bass.

The procedures outlined in Table 5–2 may be applied to any stopped note on any string, so long as the distance between the lower and upper notes can be spanned comfortably.

VIBRATO

A new dimension is added to the basic string tone with the techniques of vibrato. When correctly used, vibrato is capable of imbuing the tone with a wide range of expressive shadings. In combination with well-developed bowing techniques, the vibrato creates the "singing tone" that characterizes the mature and polished string sound.

The shadings or nuances provided by the vibrato result when the basic frequency of a pitch is modulated by slightly lowering it, then raising it. This cycle is completed by rolling, flexing, or pivoting the fingertip backward and forward on the string, creating a periodic pitch variation. When the oscillations are quick enough, the ear does not readily perceive the pitch change.

There is more than one type of string vibrato, and several methods for teaching it. Yet the mature vibrato, no matter what type, will always have the following features:

1. a coordinated motion of arm, hand, and fingers
2. rhythmic evenness
3. continuity from note to note
4. varying degrees of expressiveness
5. controlled relation to musical context

Types of Vibrato

Each of the types listed here will produce an acceptable vibrato. However, at the artist level, the performer has mastered all types and will choose one over another to achieve a special musical effect—or a combination of types for another effect. Thus, the most desirable vibrato is not a single type, but one that contains a balanced mixture of the best elements from all types.

Violin/viola. *Arm vibrato:* The forearm, wrist, and hand move backward and forward as a *single unit.* The pitch variations are created by the slight rolling and/or flexing of the fingertip in a motion that is almost parallel to the string.

Hand vibrato: In the backward and forward motion, the hand hinges at the wrist, giving the hand a somewhat faster and wider motion. In this type, there is considerably more flexing of the fingertip, but less movement of the forearm.

Cello/string bass. Because of the position of the thumb (centered on the neck, under the second finger) and the angle of the fingers to the strings (almost perpendicular), the backward and forward motion is essentially *rotory.* In this type, the forearm, wrist, and hand move as a single unit —but in a sideways, rolling motion with the fingertip pivoting on the string. For the string bass, the motion is somewhat slower and wider, with more forearm movement. In the higher positions, elements of arm vibrato and the slight flexing of the fingertip may be used.

Class versus Private Instruction

Teaching vibrato in the class situation has some drawbacks, and the decision to introduce it should be based on the following considerations:

1. Time factor: Teaching vibrato requires a good deal more class time for *personal* instruction and attention than any other technique.
2. Ability: Attempting to undertake the instruction of vibrato without the ability to demonstrate its physical mechanics may have damaging consequences. When its motion is taught incorrectly, and its execution has become ingrained, a faulty vibrato is next to impossible to repair. If you cannot demonstrate

the correct concepts with reasonable facility, it is far better to dispense with vibrato instruction altogether, refer your students to a qualified private teacher, and use the time for perfecting other techniques.

When and How to Introduce Vibrato

For the young student, the vibrato provides the first real opportunity for projecting the subtle gradations of tonal beauty at a *personal and individual* level. While the possession of a beautiful vibrato is a very desirable attribute, and one whose development should be encouraged, when and how it is introduced is critical for two reasons. First, the talented student may become discouraged if vibrato is not presented soon enough. Secondly, placing undue emphasis on its attainment can cause more harm than good—especially if it is introduced at too early a stage of development. Vibrato may be introduced when the following prerequisites have been fulfilled:

1. Bow control: With the concentration now being directed to the left hand, an uncontrolled bow not only inhibits the development of vibrato, but creates *new* bowing problems.
2. Reliable intonation: Vibrato must never be used as a camouflage for faulty intonation.
3. Shifting and positions: At this point, students have already gained some experience with the hand in motion. In the early stages, vibrato is more successfully performed in the third position, where the arm, hand, and fingers are more comfortably situated.

To insure that the focus of attention is on the left hand, initial vibrato studies should begin without the bow. Bowing and vibrato should be combined when the correct motion of the left hand has been stabilized.

Once the basic motions of the vibrato have been explained and demonstrated, working with and listening to each student *individually* becomes essential.

Violin/Viola

1. Place the violin or viola in the first rest position—under the right elbow. In this position the arm, thumb, and fingers are relaxed and more clearly visible.
2. Start with the hand in third position, placing the pad of the thumb on the side of the neck with the tip of the second finger touching the string *lightly*. The side of the index finger should be as close to the neck as possible, but *without touching it*. The remaining fingers are off the fingerboard, but over the strings.
3. The vibrato's backward and forward motion occurs as the hand pivots on the thumb. This may be established in two ways: a) *arm vibrato*—the motion is created by moving the arm and hand as an entire unit with no bending at the wrist; b) *hand vibrato:* the main motion is confined to the hand by allowing it to hinge at the wrist. In both cases, the fingertip moves to and fro as if it were "polishing" the string. Allow a wide latitude of motion here; it will help the student to feel the pivotal function of the thumb.
4. When this motion can be sustained rhythmically and evenly, gradually increase the fingertip pressure until it touches the fingerboard. The tip now remains anchored but flexible on its contact points—with no sliding. If the motion is correct and the thumb and fingertip are relaxed, there will be a slight *flexing* of the first joint of the finger—slightly below the pitch on the backward cycle and resuming normal pitch and position at the end of the upward cycle (see Figures 5–32 and 5–33). So long as the motions remain rhythmic and even, the speed of the oscillations may be gradually increased.
5. Continue these procedures on all strings with the remaining fingers. Use a 2–3–1–4 finger sequence.
6. Repeat Steps 2–5 in the *playing position*—still without the bow. If the motion cannot be sustained in

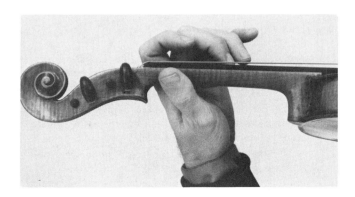

Figure 5–32. Normal finger position.

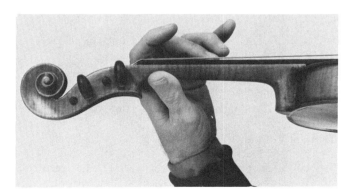

Figure 5–33. Flexed finger position. Note the flexing of the first joint in the second finger of the vibrato cycle.

this position, it is often helpful to rest the scroll of the instrument against a wall. This procedure relieves the left hand and arm from their supporting function, freeing them for vibrato movements only.

Cello/String Bass

Most of the statements contained in the procedures for violin and viola vibrato have application here. Such conditions as correct hand, arm, and finger position; relaxed attitude; and rhythmic evenness apply to all string instruments. However, because of the way the lower instruments are held, certain preparatory techniques are not used.

1. Since the main support of the cello and string bass is provided by the end pin and body, the arm and hand are already in a more advantageous position for vibrato than are the violin and viola. A preparatory stage is unnecessary, and early instruction begins with the instruments in the playing position.

2. Start with the hand in the third position, placing the pad of the thumb under the center of the neck, with the tip of the second finger on the string. In the

early stages, the thumb may be lifted away from the neck to encourage a relaxed finger and arm motion.

3. In contrast to the violin and viola mechanism, the backward and forward movements of the cello and string bass vibrato are produced by a rotary motion of the arm and hand, both functioning as a single unit. This motion causes the fingertip to pivot or roll from side to side, producing the pitch variations. There should be no bending of the wrist or flexing of the fingertip.

4. As with the violin and viola, the speed of the oscillations may be increased if the basic motion is correct and rhythmically even.

All Instruments

Once the hand has become accustomed to the oscillating motion, bowing and vibrato may be combined. Using sustained bow strokes, start with slower values (half or quarter notes), giving one value to each backward or forward motion (see Exercise 5–30). Gradually decrease the length of time between oscillations by using shorter values (eighths, triplets, sixteenths, etc.).

EXERCISE 5–30

The symbol ˅ on the note stem represents the oscillations away from the normal pitch and position.

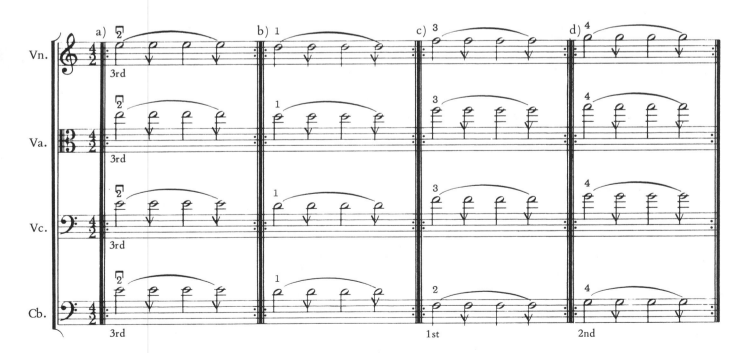

Exercise 5–30 continues

Practice the following rhythms on each string and in different positions.

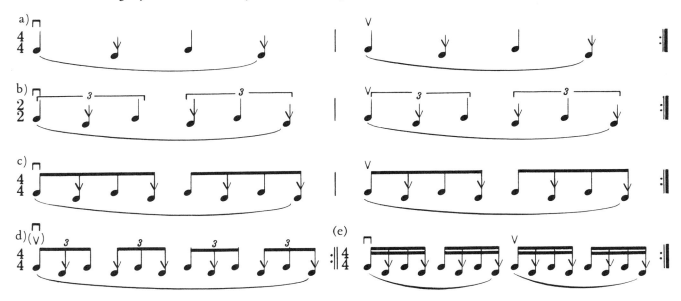

During class and private instruction, you will soon discover that some students develop a beautiful and sustained vibrato rather quickly and with the minimum of assistance. For others, it will be a struggle to develop any vibrato at all. Vibrato is a very challenging technique, one that should be nurtured slowly. Do not assume that it can be acquired—let alone mastered—in a short time.

Speed and Width of Vibrato

The vibrato is not a static nuance, but one that is varied to fit personal and musical considerations. Even a perfectly executed vibrato becomes monotonous when it is used constantly with the same degree of intensity.

In advanced applications, the intensity of the vibrato can be controlled by subtle changes in the width and speed of its oscillations. Determining the type and amount of vibrato to use is largely an individual matter, but a great deal can be learned by listening to contemporary performers. While the ability to control these two factors automatically is a very advanced skill, talented students should be aware of the possibility of varying speed and width when the basic motion of the vibrato has been mastered.

BOWING CONVENTIONS AND GENERAL PRINCIPLES OF FINGERINGS

As the director of a string program, you will find that the printed bowings in part music may be either too advanced for your ensemble or just musically awkward. To insure greater uniformity and bring about better performances, you should have a working knowledge of some of the common and generally accepted bowing conventions, symbols, and principles of fingerings if reediting is indicated.

Planning and editing bowings and fingerings require as much art as science. However, the basis of these techniques cannot be presented definitively in the scope of this work. When bowing techniques are combined with melodic, rhythmic, and dynamic elements, the variations of articulations are almost infinite. The reader is cautioned that the listings presented here can only be generalities that are subject to exceptions—not fixed or rigid prescriptions. Mastery in these areas can be achieved only through additional study, application, and experience.

Bowing Conventions

The choice of an appropriate bowing is always based on practical and musical considerations. In addition to the level of advancement of your ensemble, bowing conventions must be interpreted within the framework of the following *musical* considerations:

1. composer and historical style period
2. general character of the composition
3. level of difficulty
4. tempo
5. dynamic levels

Articulation marks. The *slur* and *phrase mark* must not be confused. The slur is interpreted literally: all the notes under it are to be played in one bow direction. The length of the slur must be conditioned by the ability of the player. At the beginning level, two-, three-, and four-note slurs are acceptable. Slurring more notes in one bow should be reserved for more advanced players.

To sustain a high volume of sound, long slurs at the f and ff levels should be avoided, unless the tempo is at least moderately fast. Longer slurs at lower dynamic levels are generally quite effective. In the use of the slur, consideration should also be given to the amount of string crossing involved and the possibility of editing slurs in such a way that a shift to another position may be made between bow changes.

A *dot* over a note indicates the relative shortening of the original value. Dotted notes may be executed in two ways: 1) *staccato*—played on the string with space (rest) between each note; 2) *spiccato*—played off the string with a bouncing stroke. Unfortunately, there is no absolute way of determining which style of bowing to use when the dots are present. But the five points given earlier will help in guiding your choice.

A *dash* over a note is used to indicate a smoother or broader style of bowing. If used with separate strokes, the dash implies that the connection between bow strokes should be as inaudible as possible. When used in combination with a slur, it gives the effect of a smooth separation between notes.

Wedges (▼) or consecutive accent marks over a note are used to indicate a very marked and detached articulation at the f and ff levels. This indication usually calls for the martelé stroke. It may also suggest the use of consecutive down-bow strokes.

Amount of bow. The length of bow used to play detached notes must be in proportion to the length of the note and speed of tempo. Generally, whole-bows are used for whole- and half-notes, with decreasing amounts for successively shorter values.

Repeated bowings. Repetition of a bowing pattern is important—especially for young and inexperienced players—because it reinforces the physical sensation of the bowing movement. When successive measures contain a repeated pattern, begin each measure with the same bow direction. Repeated bowings are more successfully performed because their cyclic pattern is predictable.

Crescendo/decrescendo. The motion of the bow toward and away from its heaviest part is used to control these dynamic shadings. When the notes for the *crescendo* are slurred in one bow, it is usually performed up-bow. The reverse (starting down-bow) is true for the *decrescendo*. If either dynamic is to be performed with separate bows, they are executed by increasing or decreasing the length, speed, or weight of the bow stroke.

Up-beats. Up-beats and most unaccented notes are played up-bow. In an up-beat pattern consisting of two or more notes, the direction of the bow should be such that the *down-beat* following is played with a down-bow. However, if an up-beat is *tied* over the barline, it is played down-bow.

Down-beats. Down-beats are usually executed with the down-bow. In cases where syncopation or shifted accents are present, the down-beat may be performed with an up-bow. For example,

After-beats. Depending upon the dynamic indication, the after-beats may be performed in a number of ways: 1) consecutive down-bows for f and ff; 2) consecutive up-bows for p and pp; and 3) as they come (⊓ – ∨) for moderate dynamic levels.

Uneven rhythmic figures. Rhythmic figures of uneven note values are often linked together in one bow direction. This is done to prevent the shortest value in the figure from being needlessly accented. Depending upon the type of articulation desired, the shortest value may be assigned a dot or dash.

Syncopation. Syncopated figures may be played as the bowing comes; or if stronger emphasis is desired, the bowing is arranged so that the longest value in the figure is played with a down-bow.

Successive down-bows. At the dynamic levels of f and ff, and when a very sharp attack is desired, successive notes may be played with a down-bow. The strokes are played in approximately the same part of the bow, but it must be retaken in a counterclockwise motion between strokes.

Successive up-bows. This type of stroke occurs most frequently at the p and pp levels and is used mainly for its clear and delicate effect. Here, the bow must be retaken in a clockwise motion between strokes.

Chords. In ensemble music, chords are generally played with successive down-bows, unless the term *divisi* is present —in which case they are played with separate down- and up-bow strokes. If played *non divisi*, be sure that the note preceding the chord is played with an up-bow.

General Principles of Fingerings

Unlike bowing conventions—which can be learned by the advanced conducting student without playing a string instrument—choosing appropriate fingerings is a highly technical skill that requires a consummate knowledge of the fingerboard, positions, and shifting. Frequently, the orchestral conductor will leave this aspect of string playing to the performer or concertmaster.

However, there are some general principles that the director of a school string program should consider when seeking a solution to a problem created by an awkward passage. Again, the reader is cautioned to interpret the following remarks as suggestions or guides only. The serious student, however, is encouraged to consult professional string players and qualified private teachers to gain a more complete understanding of this skill.

Use of open strings. Excessive use of open strings creates a more metallic tone than stopped strings and also prevents the use of vibrato. Open strings may be used only if one or more of the following conditions are present:

1. when the note after the open string is *higher*
2. with relatively shorter note values
3. contained in a double stop or chord

String crossings. Passages containing several string crossings can cause bowing problems. They may be simplified and improved by one or more of the following:

1. greater use of the fourth finger for violin and viola
2. playing the passages in different positions
3. use of extended first and fourth fingers

Shifting. When a shift is required, plan its placement so

that at least two notes may be played in that position before another shift is initiated. In addition to this point, there are other conditions where a shift is more easily or accurately executed:

1. on the half-step or next smallest interval
2. between bow changes
3. on shorter note values

Maintaining tone color. In rather slow and expressive passages, the tone color should be preserved by playing the passage in different positions *on the same string.* Also, when different sections of the ensemble are playing the same melodic line, the fingerings should be kept as uniform as possible.

Trills. The fingerings must be planned so that the trill will be executed with combinations of the *stronger* fingers. Unless absolutely necessary, but with the exception of the string bass, the fourth finger must be avoided when performing trills.

FINGERING CHARTS
FINGERING CHART FOR VIOLIN

Accidentals are not included in this chart. Listing all possible combinations of notes with sharps and flats would be redundant because a note one chromatic half-step higher or lower (than those given on the chart) would generally be played with the same finger.

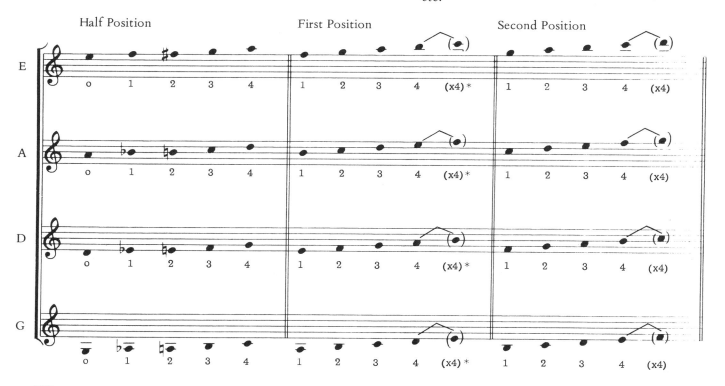

*The fourth finger extension (X4) should be used only when: a) the extension note lies a half-step higher than a regular fourth-finger note; b) the succeeding note is lower than the extended note; and c) the tempo is slow enough to permit effective use.

FINGERING CHART FOR VIOLA

Accidentals are not included in this chart. Listing all possible combinations of notes with sharps and flats would be redundant because a note one chromatic half-step higher or lower (than those given on the chart) would generally be played with the same finger.

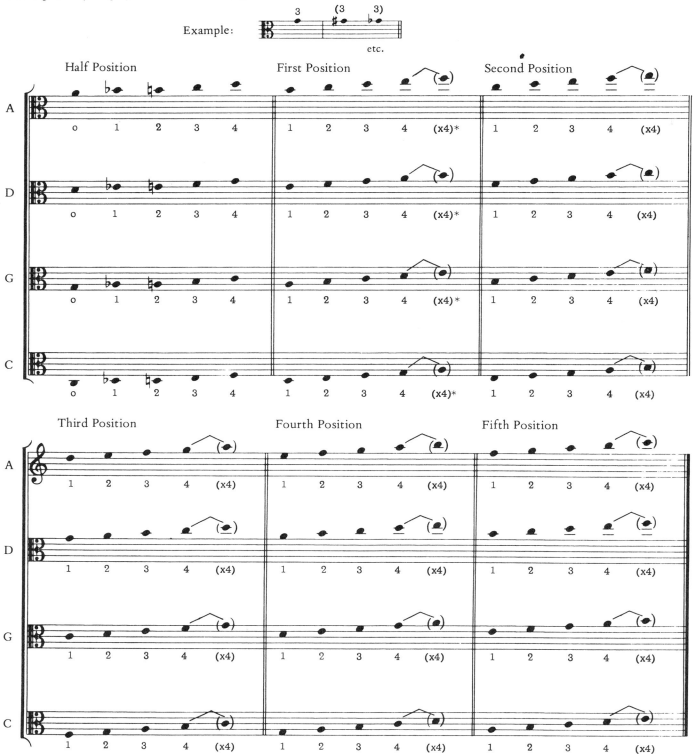

*The fourth finger extension (X4) should be used only when: a) the extension note lies a half-step higher than a regular fourth-finger note; b) the succeeding note is lower than the extended note; and c) the tempo is slow enough to permit effective use.

FINGERING CHART FOR CELLO

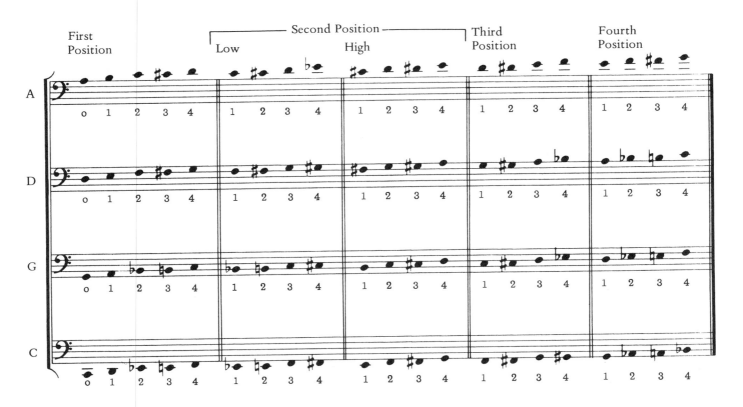

FINGERING CHART FOR STRING BASS

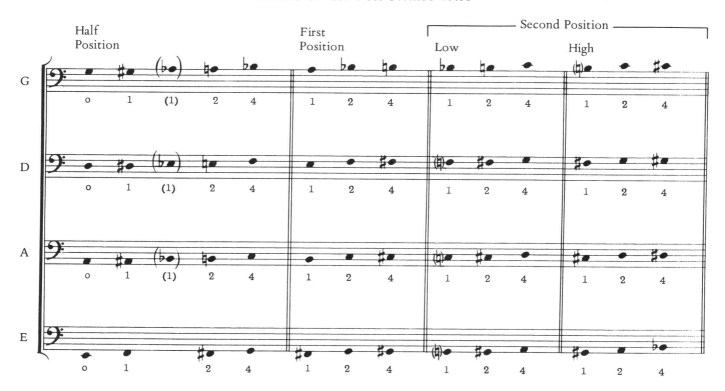

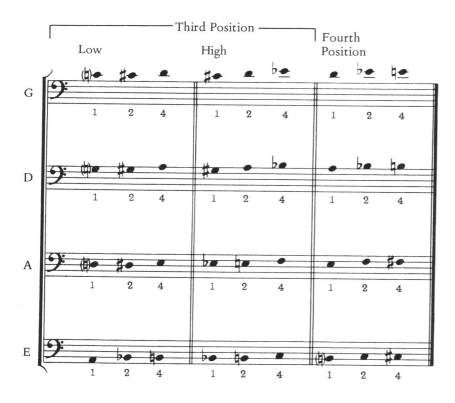

140

EXERCISES FOR EDITING BOWINGS AND FINGERINGS

The exercises in this section will provide practical experience in editing bowings and fingerings. As you edit the selections, refer to the earlier sections of this chapter on "Bowing Techniques, Scales, and Arpeggios," "Bowing Conventions and General Principles of Fingerings," and "Fingering Charts." In addition to tempo descriptions, implications of meter, and dynamic indications, there are other points that should be given equal consideration:

1. The music itself is always the overriding factor in planning bowings and fingerings. The fingerings and articulations indicated by your bowings must compliment, reinforce, and preserve the style and character of the composition.

2. Before editing begins, each section of the composition must be analyzed. Look for those theoretical elements that may *predict* certain fingerings, bow directions, and/or patterns: phrase endings and beginnings, the crescendo and diminuendo, the fermata, syncopation, unusually rapid dynamic changes, etc.

3. While some indications may appear to be obvious, do not limit your choices. Let your final version reflect the best possible solution after several attempts.

4. The indication of a particular bowing, fingering, or position must always take into account your students' level of advancement. Whatever the indication, it should improve the playability and musicality of the passage—not make it more difficult.

5. In the case of printed bowings and fingerings, if your students are having difficulty in performing them accurately or they seem inappropriate, alternatives must be considered—but only if they are compatible with the intent of the music.

6. Where applicable, keep the bowings and fingerings consistent between the various sections of the ensemble, especially when the melodic contours are identical.

EXERCISE 5-31. EXCERPT FROM *DIDO AND AENEAS* (NO. 34)

Purcell

EXERCISE 5–32. EXCERPT FROM THE *CLOCK SYMPHONY*, FIRST MOVEMENT

Haydn

EXERCISE 5–33. EXCERPT FROM *SYMPHONY NO. 5,* SECOND MOVEMENT

Schubert

EXERCISE 5–34. EXCERPT FROM *EGMONT OVERTURE,* OP. 84

Sostenuto, ma non troppo

Beethoven

Chapter 6

INTERMEDIATE CHAMBER MUSIC SELECTIONS

The selections in this chapter extend and amplify the concepts presented in the previous chapter. Here you will have the opportunity to apply and synthesize those techniques in a musical context. Each selection contains one or more of the techniques introduced in the previous chapter: bowing, fingerings, shifting, chords, etc.

The examples are drawn from the main style periods; and the bowings are, for the most part, as indicated by the composer. Others have been carefully edited to preserve the style and character of the composition. In addition to standard orchestral procedures, there are examples of contemporary string techniques.

In some examples, fingerings are indicated in two versions: one for first position, the other for position work. Where practical, both versions should be played. While the first-position version may be easier for younger players, changing positions contributes to the musicality of the

composition by avoiding unnecessary open strings and string crossings.

Explanation of the Symbols

1. Alternate fingerings are indicated in parentheses.
2. Extensions are indicated by an "X" preceding a finger number (X2 or X4).
3. An extended line after a finger number indicates that the finger is to remain down until the end of the line (3———).
4. A □ on a line or space indicates a preparatory finger on an adjacent string.
5. Positions are indicated with arabic numerals (2nd, 3rd, etc.).

AMERICA, THE BEAUTIFUL

EXCERPT FROM *SYMPHONY NO. 104,* FIRST MOVEMENT

Haydn

EXCERPT FROM *CONTRA DANSE*

Beethoven

EXCERPT FROM THE *"UNFINISHED" SYMPHONY,* FIRST MOVEMENT

Schubert

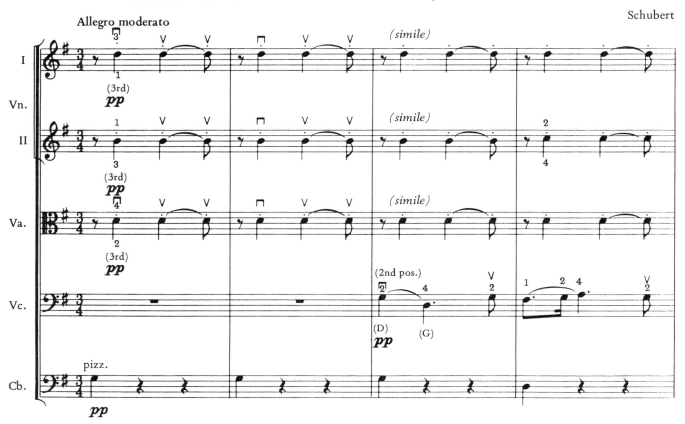

EXCERPT FROM *SYMPHONY NO. 1,* FOURTH MOVEMENT

Brahms

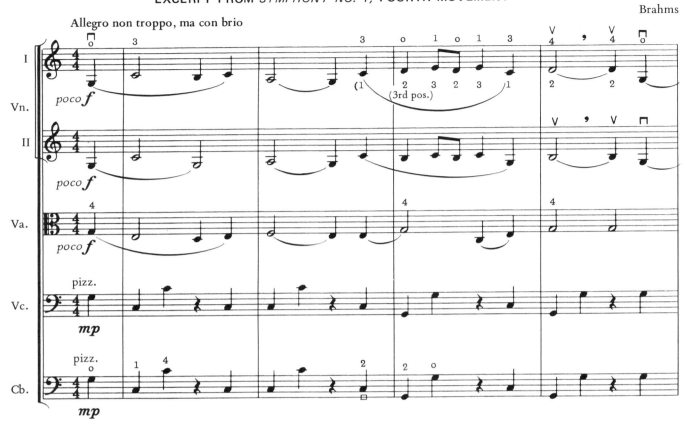

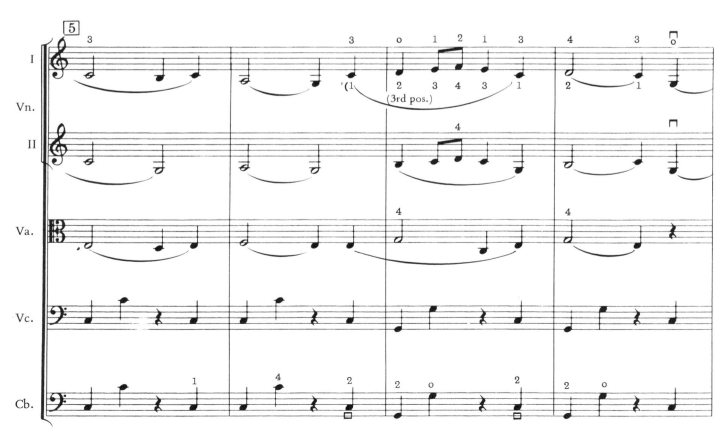

EXCERPT FROM *VOCALISE*, OP. 34, NO. 14

Rachmaninoff
Arr. Oddo

Chapter 7

THE EFFECTIVE STRING PROGRAM IN THE SCHOOLS

At the elementary level and in some secondary schools, the string teacher may be assigned to several different locations in the system, spending full days at one or more schools, and fractional days at others. The number of schools serviced by the string teacher will depend primarily on budget and enrollment, and secondarily on the prevailing attitudes of administrators, faculty, and parents toward the need for a string program.

The task of a traveling teacher contains challenges that are somewhat different from the instructor who is assigned to a permanent location. If you are assigned to several schools, remain flexible and be able to adapt to changing situations. But do this without becoming anonymous. Creating and sustaining an effective string program requires an enthusiastic and qualified teacher with the ability to work harmoniously with a number of people. The rapport you develop between you and your colleagues, the parents, and the community is just as important as that developed between you and your students. If your schedule conflicts with the other music instructors in the school system —and this happens often—make it a point to meet with them periodically (when it is mutually convenient) to outline your goals and seek their assistance. Discuss how strings can be integrated into existing ensembles, how they may be used to enhance the total music program, and how to make them compatible with the overall objectives of a humanistic education.

Whether you are assigned to a single school or have to travel to different locations, your main function will always be to *create and sustain* an interest in strings. Within this dual role there are the responsibilities of recruitment; class scheduling; purchases of instruments, music, equipment, etc. Some of these responsibilities will be discussed here in detail. Others, because they are qualified by variables that you cannot control—budgets, facilities, scheduling—are presented as suggested procedures only.

RECRUITING STRING STUDENTS

Experienced string teachers have developed a number of different methods for recruiting students.* While each may

*See Appendix D, "Recruitment and Public Relations," p. 184.

be valid for its individual teaching situation, no single approach can be prescribed as the most successful for all situations. Often, the success of the recruiter is the result of combining the best aspects of a number of approaches.

Preparing for Recruiting

After outlining some very clear objectives, goals, and programs, here are three specific possibilities for laying the groundwork for recruiting:

1. Gain the cooperation of as many potential supporters as possible: administrators, faculty, parent/teacher associations, students, alumni, etc.
2. Request public-service announcements from local newspapers, radio, and television stations.
3. Contact local and national instrument dealers. Request assistance through suggestions, posters, displays, films, and recruiting materials.

When to Recruit

Communities interested in providing well-balanced musical experiences for their children should be made aware that to develop a successful string program, participation must occur earlier for the string player than for any other type of musical activity. If, for example, a symphony or chamber orchestra is their desire, neither could exist at the junior-high or high-school levels without a well-organized elementary-level string program.

Ideally, the recruiting program should begin at the third or fourth grade levels, during the first few weeks of the fall term. During this period of a few weeks, start your recruiting as early as possible—before the students have committed their free periods to other activities.

In other school systems, students may not begin an instrument until the sixth grade. This is becoming more common because of the increasing number of intermediate (middle) schools. In such systems, it is suggested that some type of prerecruitment should occur in the spring term for the fifth graders.

Recruiting Techniques

Before specific approaches are discussed, there are several features that should be incorporated into any recruiting presentation:

1. During a recruitment session, be positive, enthusiastic, cheerful. Students rarely make a differentiation between liking an activity and liking the teacher. In the beginning, you are selling yourself—not an instrument.

2. Emphasize music as a *social* experience. Even young students have the impression that to play a string instrument requires hours and hours of dull practice and drill, sacrifice, and isolation from their friends. Highlight some of the extracurricular activities the student will be involved in because they can play an instrument.

3. Depending on the ages of the students and the number and sizes of instruments available, try to recruit for all instruments. Before a presentation, have all instruments ready to show—violin, viola, cello, and string bass. In this way the students will know that everyone will not be playing the same instrument—they have a choice!

4. If your teaching situation permits, ask current members of a student string ensemble to assist in the presentation. It is much easier for prospective students to "picture" themselves actually playing an instrument, than when viewing members of a string quartet from a local symphony or university. Where possible, allow the prospective students to directly experience playing an instrument. One suggestion is to let them strum (*à la* guitar) a rhythmic pattern on the open strings while the advanced ensemble performs a simple melody.

5. In planning a presentation, select musical examples that contain short and catchy melodies. Use familiar melodies: popular tunes, television theme music and jingles, etc. Also, ask your performers to dress casually.

6. Children are fascinated with some of the special techniques used on string instruments. Select a short tune that the children know—their classroom teacher can suggest one—and play it in a set of variations using pizzicato, tremolo, *col legno,* and *sul ponticello.*

7. After a presentation is given, don't ask "How many students want to play the violin?" but rather, ask *individual* students "What instrument do you think you'd like to play?" or "Would you like to play the violin?" ". . . the cello?" and so on.

8. At the conclusion of a recruiting session, give each student a letter directed to his or her parents. The letter should contain the following types of information:
   a. Optional: a brief biography listing your qualifications, teaching experience, and educational preparation.
   b. Your school room number, and office and home phone numbers.
   c. A detailed review of your recruitment presentation: goals and objectives, what you hope to achieve, opportunities for the children, etc.
   d. How instruments and music will be provided for the children.
   e. The date, time, and place for the first class meeting. Invite parents to attend.
   f. In terms of long-range opportunities for their children, point out to the parents that at most colleges and universities, qualified string players are given a very high priority in obtaining scholarships.

Two Approaches to Recruiting

"Mini" lesson. Since our main objective is to get students to enjoy the experience of making music by playing an instrument—as quickly as possible—the "mini" lesson is an extremely effective recruiting approach. As the description implies, a short lesson is given to a number of interested students, either in their classroom or at an informal meeting in the rehearsal room where the parents can observe. So that each student receives maximum attention, the number of children per lesson should be limited to between 4 and 6.

The success of this approach stems from the one-to-one relationship between the string teacher and student. For the child, the experience is immediate because of the instant participation and direct involvement. In this approach, the students convince themselves right from the start that playing a string instrument is not difficult and can be fun.

The little song given in Example 7-1 may be used for the "mini" lesson. Since *Marching* contains mostly open strings and first finger, it can be learned very quickly—even by first graders. Place the information shown in Figure 7-1. on the chalkboard and ask the students to join in as you sing and point to the letters of the open strings and finger numbers of the song.

After some preliminary explanations of the names of the strings, how to hold the instrument and bow, play pizzicato, draw the bow, and set the first finger on the D string, teach the children to play *Marching* by rote—first pizzicato, then arco. When recruiting children from the later grades, the title *Marching* may seem a bit childish and should be used with discretion. You may substitute a new title that is more appropriate to the age of the students: *March in D* is one possible substitute.

Student musicale. In this approach to recruiting, student string players from an existing ensemble, or those invited from a neighboring school system, present an informal lecture/demonstration. In the course of the presentation, the *members of the ensemble* can explain the parts of the instruments, describe how tone is produced, show the dif-

EXAMPLE 7-1. *MARCHING*

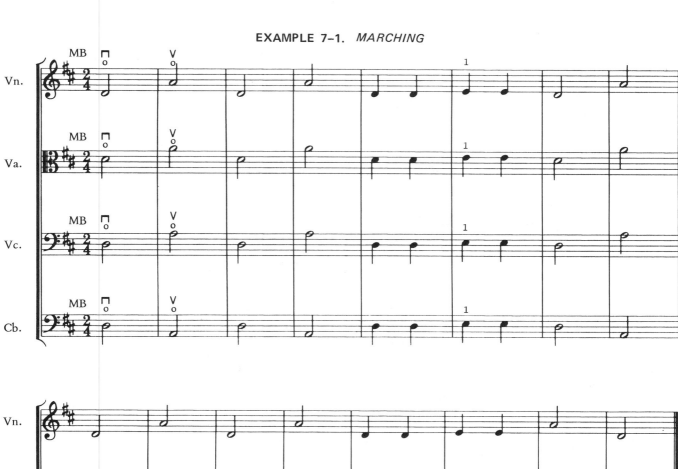

Figure 7-1. Tablature Notation of *Marching*.

Table 7–1. Relation between Instrument Sizes, Grade, and Age Levels.

Grade (Age) Levels	Violin*	Viola*	Cello*	Bass
Grade 4 (9)	1/2, 3/4	13", 14"	1/2, 3/4	1/2
Grade 5 (10)	1/2, 3/4	13", 14"	1/2, 3/4	1/2
Grade 6 (11)	3/4, 4/4	14", 15"	3/4, 4/4	1/2
Grades 7 and up (12 and up)	3/4, 4/4	15" and up	3/4, 4/4	1/2, 3/4**

*In Suzuki instruction, violins are available in 1/16, 1/10, and 1/8 sizes; cellos in 1/8 and 1/4 sizes.
For smaller violas, a 3/4 violin may be restrung with thin-gauged viola strings.
**The standard size professional bass is a 3/4; 4/4 sizes are rarely used.

ferent sizes of the instruments, demonstrate the characteristic timbres of each, and tell the children some of their experiences in music.

During the performance, be sure that the music contains several different types of articulations: pizzicato, tremolo, etc. Seat the children as close to the performers as possible —even on the floor surrounding the musicians. Let the performers ask the children such questions as "Which instrument sounds the highest?" ". . . the lowest?" "Which instrument is playing the melody?" and so on.

This student-to-student approach is very successful as a recruiting technique because of the obvious peer identification. After the presentation, set aside some time so that the children, performers, and you will have a chance to meet and talk with each other.

Selecting Students

Some string teachers encourage the use of a testing/ screening program for selecting students. While it would be ideal to work solely with children who have a demonstrated "talent" or potential for music, *any* child who expresses an interest in playing a string instrument must be given every opportunity to develop his musical skills. There are always *individual* students who, because of their initiative and desire to progress, succeed at a rate equal to or greater than that predicted by a testing/screening program. Excluding a child from a program on the basis of such an approach contradicts the genuine objectives and goals of music in the schools. Testing should be used for diagnostic purposes only, that is, to determine how you can help the student to overcome specific areas of weakness.

In selecting students, the only decision you should have to make is pairing the right instrument with the right student. Most children have no difficulty in adjusting to the violin or viola if the correct size instrument is selected. However, if a child expresses an interest in playing the cello or string bass, there are certain physical prerequisites to

look for in the student's left hand. Because of the longer string lengths of these instruments, the length of the fourth finger and general span between all fingers should be such that they can comfortably cover all the notes in first position.

CLASS PROCEDURES AND SCHEDULING

Choosing the Correct Size Instrument

The instrument chosen for a student must always be in proportion to the student's physical stature. The figures given in Table 7–1 list and compare the different size instruments with student grade (age) levels. This information may alleviate some of the problems of selection but, because of physical differences and growth rates between students, it may not be the most reliable method.

The most accurate method for selecting the correct size instrument is to "fit" each student with at least two different size instruments. With the instrument in the playing position, here are the points to observe in this approach:

Violin/viola. If the student can extend his left arm so that the fingertips can curl over the scroll *into the peg box*, the instrument is large enough (see Figures 7-2 and 7-3).

Cello. With the left hand in the correct playing position, the student should be able to comfortably span the interval of a minor third between the first and fourth fingers.

String bass. With the left hand in the correct playing position, the student should be able to comfortably span the interval of a major second between the first and fourth fingers.

Figure 7-2. Incorrect size.

Figure 7-3. Correct size. Compare the distance between the elbow and back of instrument and the fingers on the scroll.

Homogeneous or Heterogeneous Groupings

Teaching strings in the classroom can be approached from two basic directions: forming classes of like instruments—*homogeneous*—or mixed instruments—*heterogeneous*. Both approaches have their distinct advantages and disadvantages; and where the teaching situation is flexible, a balanced use of both will produce the greatest results.

Generally, homogeneous groupings are used at the elementary levels, where students should not be distracted by conflicting sounds or instructions. Also, because of unison melodies, progress is quite rapid. As the students gain facility, they should be moved into a heterogeneous group. This move is usually made prior to the junior high level. Because of the different instruments, the students in a heterogeneous grouping are exposed to varying tonal qualities, expanded ranges, greater sonorities, part playing, and ensemble practices and experiences.

While the freedom to choose one type of grouping over the other would be ideal, the actual approach used may be dictated by extramusical considerations: budgetary restrictions, scheduling, maintaining minimum class sizes, number of instruments, and so forth.

Seating Plan

The most practical class seating (or standing) plan depends on the size of the class, variety of instruments, and the shape and size of the classroom. Whichever plan is chosen, there should be a minimum spacing of four to five feet between students, and the floor in the playing area should be clear of all music stands, coats, books, cases, etc. These considerations will permit easy access to the students to assist them and prevent careless accidents. A desirable plan is one that permits the student to observe other students—and not the instructor alone.

Use of Class Time

Your most important contribution to building a string program will occur during class instruction and ensemble rehearsals. During this time, attempt to create a cheerful classroom atmosphere and be generous with praise and attention—these are among the best motivators. To help you make this time efficient, creative, and productive, here are some suggested techniques for teaching:

1. Keep all explanations short and to the point. Do a lot of reviewing and encourage questions.
2. Demonstrate each new technique. Use rote and pizzicato approaches for new left-hand techniques, and be sure that your demonstration can be seen by all students.
3. Move around the classroom frequently so that you can adjust left- and right-hand positions. Be personable with each child; use first names, and avoid embarrassing the students.
4. No matter the level of advancement, encourage stu-

dents to compose and perform their own compositions.

5. In a heterogeneous class, keep everyone occupied, and distribute your attention equitably. Don't drill the first violins while the other sections sit and wait. When working with one section, have the others practice their fingerings silently. Use a sectional rehearsal for drilling difficult passages.

6. In advanced groups, stimulate a greater awareness of changing timbres, balanced sonority between sections, aspects of form, etc. Encourage students to experiment with alternate ways of bowing or fingering a passage. Discuss the merits of their choices.

7. Whenever possible, look for opportunities to include historical and theoretical information within the musical experience.

8. Vary the rehearsal routine by including *short* warm-up pieces, scales and arpeggios, bowing exercises, and review material.

9. Prior to a rehearsal, ask a student with proven tuning ability to assist in checking for and correcting out-of-tune instruments.

10. Provide opportunities for groups or individuals to perform for peers, teachers, and parents.

Use of Rote Techniques

At the beginning stage, or when new bowing or fingering techniques are introduced, most problems encountered are kinesthetic in origin. So that good habit patterns of finger and bow-arm motion are developed quickly, rote procedures should be used until the new techniques have been assimilated.

As an illustration, a rote approach to teaching the beginning of *Three Blind Mice* for the violin and viola can be accomplished in two ways:

1. Saying the letter names of the pitches to be played: $C\# - B - A$ $C\# - B - B - A$, etc.
2. Saying the string name and finger numbers: (On the A string) $2 - 1 - A$ $2 - 1 - 1 - A$, etc.

Whichever approach is selected, the letternames or string names and finger numbers should be written on the chalkboard in plain view of all students.

Scheduling

The responsibility for scheduling string classes and larger ensembles usually falls to the senior member of the music faculty and/or the school administrator. Often the times and rooms available for special classes and activities have been blocked out for the entire school year, and you may have to develop your program around the needs of more established musical organizations. In some schools, the facilities may be so limited that all instrument classes and performing groups will be competing for the same rehearsal area. In other schools—because of an enlightened administration, better facilities, and a cooperative faculty—there are minimal problems in scheduling string classes.

Because scheduling practices vary so widely from school to school across the country, the information given in Table 7–2 should be interpreted as generalized recommendations only.

PURCHASING FOR THE SCHOOLS

Sustaining an effective string program has as much to do with the quality of your purchases for the schools as the talent of your students or your ability as a teacher.

The needs and priorities for purchases will change from year to year; and to insure optimum results, periodic re-evaluation of the program is essential. While some purchases require only minimal attention, those discussed here represent the main areas of concern.

Instruments

The cost of instruments will clearly constitute the largest expenditures in your program. Depending on the school's administrative philosophy, you may have little control over budgetary allocations, but you can insist that the quality of instruments purchased are at a very high level. The Music Educators National Conference (MENC) has established minimum standards for string instruments in the schools. These standards are given in Appendix A and provide a very valuable source for determining instrumental purchases.

Table 7–2. String Class Scheduling.

Level	Meetings per Week	Class Size
Elementary	2	8–10
Junior High*	3	14–16
Senior High*	4–5	18–20

*Depending on the level of advancement, these may be the Intermediate and Advanced Orchestras.

Table 7–3. Minimum Numbers and Sizes of School-Owned Instruments.

	Violin	Viola	Cello	Bass
Elementary	5 1/2* 5 3/4	3 Jr.	2 1/2 2 3/4	2 1/2
Junior High	7 3/4 7 4/4	5 Int.	3 3/4 3 4/4	2 1/2 2 3/4
Senior High	13 4/4	3 Int. 5 Stand.	7 4/4	5 3/4

*Few school systems supply the 1/8 and 1/4 size violins and cellos used in the lower grades. These are usually provided through a rental program.

School- or Student-Owned Instruments

Many schools own instruments and provide them to beginning students free of charge or rent them for a nominal fee. As the students progress, they are encouraged to purchase their own instruments. If the school system does not own instruments, or the demand exceeds the supply, students should be directed to a local music dealer for a rental instrument.

Rental plans are popular with parents because they minimize financial risk. Often dealers will rent an instrument with the understanding that the rental fee can be applied to the purchase of the rented instrument or a newer one. Renting has the added advantage of allowing the parent to delay the purchase of an instrument until their child is playing a full-sized instrument. When children are started in the early grades, for example, they may progress through 1/8, 1/4, 1/2, and 3/4 sizes before reaching a full-sized (4/4) instrument.

When parents decide to purchase an instrument, they will need your assistance if they are to receive maximum value. Provide them with some guidelines outlining the need for a properly adjusted and well-made instrument. The MENC "Minimum Standards for Stringed Instruments in the Schools"* could be used as the basis for such a guide. Tell the parents to avoid buying an instrument from a discount house or mail order firm. Give them the names and addresses of several reputable string dealers—dealers who have instruments that conform to MENC standards. Most dealers encourage students to show an instrument to their instructors before a purchase is concluded. Examine the instrument for quality and condition, then make your recommendations.

Numbers, Sizes, and Types of Instruments

The information given in Table 7–3 represents an "ideal" balance between numbers, sizes, and types of instruments at three levels of instruction. Ultimately, the size of enrollment in your school system will determine whether the figures in the table should be increased or decreased.

*See Appendix A, p. 176.

If the budget allocated to your program cannot support this ideal, it is better to supplement purchases with rentals than to compromise quality for quantity. The instruments purchased will have to service many students for several years. Over this period, cheaper instruments are often more expensive because of their greater frequency of repairs—not to mention loss of class time. When purchasing school instruments, it is most expedient to order them as complete outfits: instrument, bow, case or cover, and rosin. At the young artist level, these items are usually purchased separately.

Selecting Music

Selecting a music library that will serve the needs of individual students, beginning through advanced classes, and larger ensembles requires careful thought and planning.** The search for suitable music is often difficult and time-consuming, but the success of your program can be attributed partly to the appropriateness and quality of your selections.

One of the cardinal rules of selecting materials is *never buy music sight unseen.* Prior to purchase, all music must be examined and analyzed in terms of suitability and musical value. The time-consuming aspect of selecting suitable music can be minimized somewhat by taking advantage of the following sources:

1. Write to publishing companies that specialize in string and orchestral music. Many will send examination copies of standard and new publications. Publishers also have exhibits at local, state and regional music educators conventions. Here you can request complimentary materials and place your name on their mailing lists.
2. Establish a music exchange program with string teachers in neighboring communities so that the music libraries can be shared.

**Graded lists for class, individual, and ensemble music are given in Appendices C and D.

3. Attend concerts, music festivals, and recitals that have students and groups that are similar to your own. Here you can "audition" materials by evaluating both the level of difficulty and quality of the music.

Your selection of materials must be divided between the levels and types of instruction: method books for classes; solos, etudes and technical studies for individual instruments; and ensemble pieces. Within each category, a well-balanced library will include selections representing the main style periods, popular arrangements, and examples with contemporary compositional idioms. To help you examine and analyze a composition for suitability, here are some general questions that should be raised:

Method books

1. Does the book contain clear illustrations and directions on holding the instrument and bow, hand positions, and posture?
2. Is it organized around a logical and sequential plan that provides theoretical and technical information, musical understanding, and skills?
3. Are the fingering and hand position illustrations side-by-side?
4. Is there an adequate balance between developmental exercises and ensemble pieces?
5. Does it contain a fingering chart, list of musical terms, review and supplementary materials?

Etudes and technical studies

1. Does the volume have an appropriate balance between scales and arpeggios?
2. Are all major bowing techniques covered adequately?
3. Are double stops and chords included?
4. Are the materials arranged in a logical and progressive order?
5. Are individual exercises clearly identified by content —trill exercises, martelé exercises, etc?

Ensemble pieces

1. Does the collection have both student and audience appeal?
2. Does the music challenge the technical skill, musicianship, and reading ability of your ensemble?
3. Is the music edited well?
4. Are parts cued for other instruments?
5. Can the piece be used in a number of different circumstances and capacities—teaching or performance?

Equipment and Accessories

Keeping a well-stocked supply of back-up instruments, equipment, and accessories is an important aspect of main-

taining an effective string program. When minor repairs or the replacement of a worn part are indicated, they must be accomplished quickly.* If this is not possible, a reserve instrument should be available. Since student progress is affected by the playing condition of an instrument, their *interest* can diminish rapidly if the instrument is taken out of circulation for repairs. Generally, applying a 10 percent reserve margin for instruments and 20 percent for bows— while somewhat conservative—is a workable formula. Periodic rehairing is the main factor for the higher percentage applied to bows.

The amounts and types of other back-up equipment and accessories should be formulated by considering your operating budget, storage space, ratio between numbers of students and instruments, and other program needs. Those items most frequently in need of repair or replacement (strings, bridges, etc.) should be given the highest priority in a list of basic back-up equipment.

STORAGE FACILITIES

In school systems containing newer buildings, storage areas have been designed and integrated into a total facility and are generally quite adequate. In other schools, storage facilities may not be so ideal. Often they are scattered throughout different parts of the building. In evaluating your storage facilities, here are some questions to be raised and comments to consider if the areas are to be developed for maximum and efficient use:

1. Is the instrument storage room centrally located? Ideally, this facility should adjoin the rehearsal room so that the time needed for a student to get and return an instrument does not reduce rehearsal time.
2. Can the instruments be stored in individual and locked compartments? As opposed to open shelving or hall lockers, this type of storage provides maximum security, and simplifies the issuing, inventory, and inspection of instruments.
3. Are the instruments protected from extremes of temperature and humidity? Instruments should be stored away from heating ducts, windows, radiators, and other heating sources. In addition, there should be adequate ventilation and a means for controlling humidity. Place a hygrometer (humidity gauge) in the instrument storage room; and if the relative humidity falls below 45 percent, install an automatic, cold-air humidifier.
4. Have provisions been made for making minor instrumental repairs? Another ideal facility is to have a repair room—equipped with tools, parts, and accessories—next to the rehearsal area so that emergency repairs can be accomplished quickly.

*A list of basic supplies for repairs and adjustments of instruments is given later in this chapter, pages 170–174.

5. Does the instrumental storage room provide for easy access? This room should be accessible to students before, during, and after rehearsals. If students wish to store their instruments or pick them up, they should be able to do so without interrupting a class already in progress.

CARE AND MAINTENANCE OF INSTRUMENTS AND BOWS

There is a certain precious quality about a string instrument: it has a sense of posterity, a connection with the past, and a legacy for the future. Many of the instruments in use today by professional symphonic musicians and soloists may date back to as long ago as the late 1590s. Such instruments have passed through the centuries with little more than a few scratches. Their survival is no mystery. Obviously, all the previous owners took the precautions necessary to protect and maintain their instruments in the finest possible playing condition.

Care and maintenance of an instrument can lead to more than its preservation. An instrument that has been cared for is easier to play, more tonally responsive, and will maintain or increase in value. There are practical considerations also. A well-cared-for instrument will provide many generations with trouble-free use and beauty. A string instrument is rarely replaced by a newer model unless it has been damaged beyond repair. Although the player or school music program may wish to "trade up" to an instrument of higher *quality*, string instruments never become obsolete.

When you issue an instrument, a large part of the responsibility for its safety, care, and maintenance must be assumed by your students and their parents.

Before learning how to play, your students must first learn how to care for and handle their instruments and bows. Unnecessary damage, costly repairs, and loss of time can be avoided by checking the points that follow on the next few pages. You can help to keep the instruments in peak playing condition and prevent further damage to them by encouraging your student to report the least defect to you and having it corrected by a qualified string repairman as quickly as possible.

Care of Instruments

Protection and safety. Sudden changes or extremes in temperature will cause severe damage to a string instrument. Students must never leave an instrument in the back seat or trunk of a car; when not in use, store the instrument in an area away from heat (radiators, hot air vents), damp basements, or unheated areas. Ideally, the storage area should be at a room temperature of 68–72° with a relative humidity of 45%. Below that percentage, there is a danger of the seams cracking, warping, or opening, and of the varnish flaking.

During a pause in a class session or rehearsal, the instrument must be kept in a closed case or cover. Encourage your students to handle the instruments without touching the varnished surface. Except for the bass, the instruments may be carried with the left hand closed firmly around the fingerboard and neck. Cellos and basses should be laid on their ribs, away from the traffic patterns of the room, the end pin fully inserted into the instrument, the bow set in a safe place, and the bridge facing away from the center of the rehearsal area.

When playing begins, be sure there are no obstructions near the instruments or bows. Allow plenty of elbow room. At the conclusion of a playing session, show your class how to clean the instrument and return it to its case or cover. If a shoulder rest is used, it must be removed before the student attempts to close the case. The compartments in violin and viola cases and the pouches in cello and bass covers must never contain objects that can injure an instrument. Case and cover interiors should be vacuumed periodically. Cellists and bassists may store music in the pouches provided in their instrument covers, but violinists and violists must never attempt to stuff music in their cases. Before picking up an instrument in its case or cover, tell your students to check that all locks, latches, and snaps are secure and closed.

Cleaning. Rosin dust is an abrasive and must be removed from all parts of the instrument and bow, except for the bow hair itself. Rosin that has accumulated in the bowing area can be removed from the body of the instrument and bow shaft with a soft cloth. A flannel-like cloth is recommended and should be kept in the instrument case or cover at all times for such purposes. Clean the rosin from the strings by lightly buffing with a small piece of Triple 0 (000) steel wool (available at most hardware stores), followed by a cloth clean-up. Strings may also be cleaned with alcohol or methanol if used carefully. Whether this responsibility can be delegated to your students will depend mainly on their age. For the younger student, cleaning the strings with steel wool should be explained to the parents. The steel wool can be kept in the case in some type of container to prevent the very fine steel strands from breaking loose. Rub the fingerboard with a soft cloth to remove finger oils and rosin.

If rosin has become caked on the instrument and bow, have your repairman remove it. Do not attempt to remove it with alcohol or an alcohol-base cleaner. This chemical is a solvent and will seriously damage the varnish. Xylene, however, is fairly safe, but should be used sparingly and only after it has been tested first. A good area for testing is on the rib area around the end button. To retain luster and preserve the wood, polish the body of the instrument with a specially prepared product only.

Bridge alignment. Even on the very finest of instruments, tuning the strings will pull the top of the bridge in the direction of the scroll. At first, because the movement is so slight, it will go unnoticed. But the tilting is progressive and, if not checked and corrected frequently, the bridge will warp and eventually crack. The tilting also affects other factors. As the top of the bridge is pulled toward the scroll, the string length is shortened, correct intonation becomes difficult, and the acoustical characteristics of the instrument are compromised. Frequent inspection for bridge alignment avoids all repairs, costs, and needless time lost in correcting this problem. A bridge in proper alignment need never be replaced except for seasonal variations (see next section) in the instrument.

The bridge is out of correct alignment when the angle between the back of the bridge (the side facing the tailpiece) and the top of the instrument is not exactly 90°. To bring the bridge into perfect alignment, grasp the top of the bridge at its upper corners with the thumb and index fingers of each hand. With the instrument firmly braced, gently pull or push the top of the bridge until the 90° angle is achieved. If the bridge does not move easily, loosen the tension of all strings slightly, then reposition the bridge. Two other adjustments are necessary to keep the bridge in proper position: 1) the feet of the bridge must be centered between the *inside* notches of the F holes, and 2) the sides of the bridge must be in line with the sides of the fingerboard. Correct alignment of the last adjustment can be tested by sighting down the sides of the fingerboard from the scroll toward the edges of the bridge. To make these adjustments, follow the above procedures while moving the *feet* of the bridge, then recheck the bridge angle. When in doubt, ask a repairman to adjust the bridge properly.

Summer/winter bridges.   Seasonal changes cause instruments to expand or contract slightly. The top of the instrument swells upward in warm weather, raising the bridge and lifting the strings too high above the fingerboard. This causes the player to use more finger pressure to make the string come in contact with the fingerboard. At this time, the bridge must be replaced with one of a proper height. Save the old bridge, because in cold weather the reverse process sets in. As the instrument contracts, the bridge may be too low, and the strings will be too close to the fingerboard to allow free vibration. Strings that are consistently too low can also cause grooves in the fingerboard. The bridge saved from the warmer season should correct the problem. If not, a new bridge must be fitted. Ask your repairman to periodically check the bridge height.

The effects of expansion and contraction may be kept to a minimum by making a block constructed of several layers of cardboard wrapped in a soft cloth or wax paper. Your repairman can determine the correct thickness of the block for each instrument. When the instrument has been cleaned of all rosin and dust, slide the block under the end of the fingerboard and top of the instrument until it fits just snugly between the two. Never attempt to force it beyond this point. The block should be kept in place when the instrument is not in use, and especially when it is stored for a long period of time.

Strings.   The finest instrument cannot sound its best with old and lifeless strings or strings that have started to fray and unravel. Strings should be smooth and unbroken from the nut at the end of the fingerboard to the tailpiece. If not, they must be replaced as soon as possible. A frayed or un-raveled string will inhibit proper string vibration, cause needless intonation problems, and scratch the fingerboard.

String tuners.   When not in use, the string instrument has a tendency to drop in pitch. The reverse is quite rare and usually occurs only when the instrument has been exposed to wide temperature variations. In the course of tuning an instrument, the string tuner is used to bring the metal strings up to true pitch. After repeated tunings, the tuner can be turned no farther. To correct this, turn the tuner counterclockwise to loosen it, raise the string to approximate pitch with the *peg*, then fine-tune with the tuner. If the tuner for a violin or viola is the type that has the lever mechanism below the tailpiece, there is a danger that the level shank will gouge the top of the instrument. Check on this frequently, and correct with the procedures above. This type of tuner should be replaced with one that has the entire mechanism *above* the tailpiece. Periodically, lubricate the screw mechanism with a very small amount of oil.

Chin rests.   Due to the vibration of the instrument, the chin rest may become loose and produce a buzzing sound. To fix the chin rest firmly, insert a chin rest key into the small hole in each chin rest bar, turning both bars *alternately* to the right to tighten. Be careful that the key does not protrude beyond the opposite hole in the bar, because as you turn the key and bar, the key will gouge the wood behind it. The screw mechanism that holds the chin rest firmly to the instrument can act like a small vise. If tightened too much, it will cause the ribs under it to buckle and inflict severe structural damage to the interior of the instrument. When positioning the chin rest, do not let it touch the tailpiece; contact with it will also produce a buzzing sound.

Pegs and pegbox.   The pegs should fit perfectly in the peg holes to assure that the pegs turn smoothly and almost effortlessly when tuning. With continuous use, the holes of the pegbox wall will enlarge, making the pegs too short. The holes may also wear in an oval shape, thus reducing the gripping surface. This will cause slipping pegs, difficulties in tuning, and damage to the pegbox wall. This type of wear should be corrected only by a qualified string repairman. Forcing the pegs into the pegbox may cause hairline cracks to develop around the peg holes that severely reduce the strength of the pegbox and may cause it to split along these cracks. Pegs may also become sticky from use, causing a clicking or snapping sound when tuning. To remedy this, the pegs should be removed from the box and cleaned and treated with a compound to restore smooth turning. Check the pegs and pegbox area frequently.

Open edges and soundpost position.   The temperature and humidity variations that result in the expansion and contraction of the instrument—already noted in the section on bridge alignment—may cause two additional problems:

Open edges: if the expansions and contractions are great enough, the instrument will crack where there is least resistance: the glue. The areas most affected will be the top and back of the instrument where they are joined to the ribs (bouts). You should become suspicious that an edge has opened when an instrument makes a buzzing sound when played on the lower strings. A loose tuner, a loose chin rest or one that is touching the tailpiece will also cause a buzzing sound. Check these first. You can examine the instrument for open edges visually, or by lightly tapping the top or back of the instrument along the purfling with your knuckle. If they have become detached, you will not hear a solid sound as you tap, but a secondary click as the top or back hit the ribs. Do not neglect open edges; they will probably get larger. Have your string repairman reglue them as soon as possible.

Soundpost position: with the swelling of the top of the instrument in warm weather, the soundpost may become too short to hold its position. If it moves out of its position, the tonal characteristics will be disturbed. If the expansion of the top continues, the soundpost may fall and must be replaced by your repairman with a new one that is seasonally correct. In warm and humid weather, ask a qualified string repairman to inspect the position of the soundpost. A slight adjustment of the soundpost position may be in order.

Tail gut. In most cases, the term "tail gut" is a misnomer. The traditional tail gut is an animal derivative, and perspiration and humidity can cause it to stretch, fray, and break. Because of these undesirable characteristics, it has been replaced by a nylon strand that is unaffected by temperature and moisture and is practically indestructible. When an instrument comes equipped with the traditional tail gut, check it frequently to see that it holds the tailpiece securely. At the earliest opportunity, have it replaced with a nylon tail gut.

End pins. The end pins used to support, raise, and lower the cello and string bass may be damaged quite easily. During playing sessions, carrying either instrument with the end pin extended should be avoided. Frequently, the metal collar of the end pin mechanism may spin out of position because the thumb screw has been turned out too far. When the player attempts to turn the thumb screw to lock the end pin at a correct height, a very damaging series of events could take place: the tip of the thumb screw, rather than engaging the shaft of the end pin, crushes the wooden sleeve inside the mechansim. Noting that the end pin is not secured in position, the player may often apply excessive force to the thumb screw, either stripping the threads, bending it, or shearing it off. Periodically examine the alignment and position of the collar. When storing the cello or string bass, the end pin must be fully inserted and locked into position with the thumb screw. Keep the storage area floor clear of obstructions that could potentially damage this mechanism.

Care of the Bow

Stick. The precautions taken to insure your instrument's peak playing condition (safety/protection, temperature/humidity) apply to the bow as well. Encourage your students to treat the bow as an equal partner with the instrument. Get them to think of the bow as their "right-hand" instrument.

After each playing session, the rosin that has accumulated on the underside of the stick must be wiped off with a soft, clean cloth. Remember, rosin is an abrasive; do not rub the stick too hard. When not in use, the hair of the bow must be loosened to a point where there is still a very slight amount of tension in the stick. Hair that has been loosened excessively may cause the bow to warp or change the curvature of its sweep. The bow must always be kept in the case when not in use—not on a music stand or chair.

Hair. The microscopic edges of the bow hair will eventually wear down from playing. Rosin can no longer properly adhere to the hair, and its ability to grip the string is severely reduced. With worn hair, it becomes difficult to draw a clear and resonant tone. At that point, a string repairman will have to rehair the bow.

In warm and humid weather, the hair will often stretch, becoming too long to permit tightening to the proper tension. If, after a few days, it does not contract to its proper length, it may have to be shortened or rehaired.

Ivory tip. The tip is both decorative and functional. It adds beauty while reinforcing the fragile bow head. If the tip cracks or breaks off, the head of the bow will be structurally weakened. The tip should be repaired or replaced as quickly as possible.

Winding and thumb grip. The winding, like the ivory tip, is not merely ornamental. It provides a secure contact for the fingers with the bow and protects the wood in the bow, which would wear down in a relatively short time without it. If the winding begins to unravel, have it repaired or replaced. The most likely place for this to happen is in the area where the thumb comes in contact with the bow. For this reason, it is advisable to keep the thumbnail of the right hand fairly short. If your students can feel the nail touching the underside of the bow between the edge of the thumb grip and the edge of the frog, the nail is too long and will begin to gouge the wood. To preserve the beauty of the wood, the bow should not be handled beyond the frog and winding area.

Turn screw, eyelet, and frog. The mechanism that moves the frog for tightening and loosening the hair is susceptible to wear. The threads in either the shaft of the turn screw or the eyelet through which it passes may wear out. The eyelet is made of a softer metal than the turn screw and will usually show the first signs of wear. As it begins to wear, there are telltale signs: you may hear a clicking sound as you tighten the bow or the frog may slip. This indicates that the ridges in the turn screw are not engaging the walls of the eyelet completely. When the eyelet wears out altogether, the bow cannot be tightened, and the eyelet will have to be replaced.

The frog should move only to a forward or back position, never side to side. Properly fitted, the frog should be seated flush against the stick, but never to a point where the frog lining will wear against the wood. A half-turn of the eyelet in the proper direction will usually correct the fit. Your repairman can make this adjustment.

In summary, the use of common sense in matters of safety, and regular inspection of the instrument and bow—followed by the corrective adjustments outlined above—will keep them in proper playing condition. Finally, remember that prompt corrections of even the most minor changes or defects in your instruments or bows will prevent the needless interruptions that extensive repairs will cause to your program.

MAKING MINOR REPAIRS AND ADJUSTMENTS

From the very beginning of your string program, a careful routine of preventive maintenance should be outlined. Keeping accurate records of purchases and repairs—a calendar indicating such information as the frequency of bow rehairing, string changes, etc.—will prevent unnecessary damage and minimize costly repairs. The "String Inspection Record," "Trouble-Shooting Guide," and list of "Basic Supplies" included in this section will provide a basis for organizing such a routine.

In addition to these records and guides, there are several repair manuals available with suggestions for setting up repair facilities, supplies, and how-to-do-it instructions. (See Appendix D, "Instrumental Repairs.") These manuals are a necessary part of your repair and maintenance program. Beyond preventive maintenance, you will have to decide on the time and funds you wish to commit to a more extensive repair program.

Some of the problems in maintaining your equipment can be anticipated. The most common items needing regular attention are: condition of bow hair, replacing worn or broken strings, bridge alignment, and cleaning.

Depending on your budget and the amount of use your instruments receive, bows should be rehaired and strings changed a minimum of twice a year. Here again, accurate record keeping is very important. Routine maintenance should be scheduled at a time when the instruments are least used end of the school term, during school holidays, etc. This is also a good time for checking your inventory of instruments, accessories, and supplies. Periodic inspection of all instruments and bows by a qualified repairman will also help keep your instruments in the best possible playing condition.

Bow Rehairing

A bow is in need of rehairing when any of the following conditions are present:

1. Hair does not extend the full width of the ferrule.
2. Excessive breaking of hair.
3. Hair fails to hold rosin adequately.

4. Stretched or hanging hairs.
5. Difficulty in producing an acceptable sound at a high dynamic level.
6. Difficulty in sustaining an even tone from the frog to the tip.
7. Warped stick—if caused by an uneven distribution of bow hair.

Changing Strings and Cleaning Pegs

Strings should be changed as soon as they begin to show signs of wear or become *false.* A string is false when its pitch vacillates when bowed with even weight; or, when tuned in perfect fifths—open strings—fails to produce a perfect interval with an adjacent strings *when both are fingered.* If the fifths are not truly perfect, the interference pattern called *beats* will be heard. False strings occur because the gauge along the length of the string varies in thickness from wear or faulty materials or workmanship.

When changing strings, start with one of the middle strings, removing and replacing them one at a time. Replace the outside strings last. This method will prevent fallen bridges and/or soundposts. When replacing a string, insert the thickest end into the tailpiece notch or string tuner *first;* then the other end into the peg hole. Be sure to wind the string on the peg so that it leads over the fingerboard nut in a *straight* line. Strings must never cross over each other in the peg box. Figure 7-4 illustrates the correct

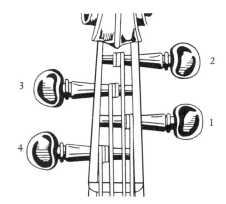

Violin	Viola and Cello*	String Bass*
1—E string	1—A string	1—G string
2—A string	2—D string	2—D string
3—D string	3—C string	3—E string
4—G string	4—G string	4—A string

*Often the two lowest strings for these instruments do not follow the same stringing sequence as the violin. That is, pegs 3 and 4 may have a reverse order for the two lowest strings, with peg 3 controlling the lowest string.

Figure 7-4. Position of strings in the pegbox.

position of the strings in the pegbox. Remember to check bridge alignment as you restring an instrument—especially after it has been tuned for the first time.

While changing strings, inspect the condition of the pegs. If they do not turn freely and smoothly, they must be removed and cleaned. Clean the peg shaft by rubbing with 000 grade steel wool, and follow this by an application of a commercial peg compound.

An instrument that has been restrung with new strings has a tendency to drop in pitch rather quickly and may take several hours before the strings will hold their designed tension. This is especially true with metal-wound-on-gut strings.

String Inspection Record

As you perform your periodic maintenance inspections, use the inspection record shown on the next page as a guide. If you cannot correct or adjust those items listed in the "No" column, copy the statements and include them with the instrument when it is sent for repair. Be sure to include full instrument identification and dates.

String Instrument Inspection Record

Prepared by Dr. Paul Van Bodegraven, Chairman, Department of Music, New York University

Published by Educational Division of Scherl & Roth, Inc.

To help you determine if your instrument is in best possible playing condition.

	Yes	No
A. PEGS		
1. Do they fit snugly in both peg hole openings?		
2. Do they turn smoothly and silently?		
3. Do they hold in position with slight inward pressure while tuning?		
B. FINGERBOARD NUT		
1. Do all strings clear fingerboard without buzzing when playing open or stopped strings?		
2. Are the string grooves in the fingerboard nut shallow?		
C. FINGERBOARD		
1. Is it smooth with no grooves?		
2. Is it glued securely on to the neck?		
3. Is it free of excess glue along edges?		
4. Is it the proper height?		
D. BRIDGE		
1. Is it the proper height?		
2. Do the feet fit perfectly with the top contour? ...		
3. Is the E string on low side of bridge (violin) A string on viola and cello, G string on bass?		
4. Is it set opposite the inside notches on the F holes?		
5. Are all string grooves shallow?		
6. Is it perfectly straight, not warped?		
7. Does it lean slightly towards the tailpiece?		
8. Is there sufficient arch so the student does not have difficulty playing from one string to the other? ..		
E. TAILPIECE		
1. Is the small end of tailpiece almost even with the outside edge of saddle?		
2. Is there some space between it and top of instrument?		
3. Is there a clearance between tailpiece and chinrest?		
F. STRINGS		
1. Are all perfectly smooth, without kinks?		
2. Is the metal winding tight?		
3. Are the adjusters on all metal strings working smoothly?		
4. Are the strings free of caked rosin?		
5. Do you have an extra set of strings in your case? .		
6. Are your reserve strings sealed from dryness?		
7. If you have any steel strings on your instrument, are they equipped with adjusters?		

	Yes	No
G. INSTRUMENT BODY		
1. Is it free from open cracks?		
2. Is the top clean and free of caked rosin?		
3. Are the front and back thoroughly glued to the ribs?		
H. THE SOUNDPOST		
1. Is it directly behind the right foot of the bridge? ..		
2. Is it perpendicular to top and back?		
3. Is the soundpost setter slot facing the right F hole?		
I. THE BOW		
1. Can it be loosened and tightened freely?		
2. Does it have enough hair?		
3. Does the hair extend the full width of the frog ferrule?		
4. Has it been rehaired in the past year?		
5. Is the bow stick free of caked rosin?		
6. Does it have real wire winding and leather thumb grip?		
7. Is the bow arch noticeable when it is tightened ready to play?		
8. Is there a protective facing, ivory or metal, on the tip?		
J. CHINREST		
1. Is the chinrest securely attached to instrument? ...		
2. Is the chinrest free of broken edges?		
3. Is it of proper height for correct posture and comfortable playing?		
K. ROSIN		
1. Do you have a full size (unbroken) cake of rosin? .		
2. Do you have a clean cake of rosin?		
3. Are you using rosin for the individual bow, i.e. (violin, cello, bass rosin)?		
L. MUTE		
1. Do you have a mute attached to your instrument ready for instant use? (Sihon mute)		
M. CELLO AND BASSES		
1. Is the adjustable endpin in proper working order? ..		
2. Do you have a cello or bass endpin rest that prevents instrument slipping while playing?		

ALL ANSWERS SHOULD BE "YES"

Instructions to correct faults of your instrument are found in repair manual, "YOU FIX THEM," published by Scherl & Roth Inc.

INSTRUMENT_____ SERIAL NO._____ DATES INSPECTED_____

1st quarter   2nd quarter

_____ _____   TEACHER_____ STUDENT NAME_____

3rd quarter   4th quarter

ADDRESS_____ TELEPHONE NUMBER_____ GRADE_____

SCHOOL_____

Trouble-Shooting Guide

Some of the problems given here have obvious solutions as to the repairs or adjustments. Others should be corrected by a qualified repairman, and such problems are identified by the asterisk (*) following the statement. This list is by no means exhaustive; it only reflects some of the more common problems faced by a string instructor. But given a good instrument to start with, a regular program of inspection, and care and maintenance, most of these problems will never occur. Keeping your equipment in the best possible playing condition may then only require bow rehairing and string changes.

Repairing Broken Bows

A broken stick may or may not be repairable. This will have to be determined by a bow repairman. If the break occurs where the head joins the stick, the repair bill may be very costly and should be undertaken only if the value of the bow warrants it. Often replacing it with a new or good-quality used bow may be the best solution.

Basic Supplies

The supplies in the following list will be sufficient for making minor repairs and adjustments. Keep these supplies

TROUBLE-SHOOTING GUIDE

A. Instruments

Problem	Possible Cause/Solution
Buzzing, rattles, etc.	1. Loose chin rest 2. Chin rest is touching side of tailpiece 3. Part of instrument is touching a button on collar or shirt, jewelry, etc. 4. Loose string tuner 5. Open seams* 6. Loose bass bar* 7. Loose purfling* 8. Loose fingerboard* 9. Strings too close to the fingerboard* 10. New crack—or an old crack has reopened* 11. Depth of string into fingerboard nut or bridge is incorrect*
Muted or metallic tone	Incorrect position of soundpost*
Difficulty in playing on single strings	Incorrect curvature of bridge and/or spacing of strings on bridge*
Strings too high over fingerboard	Bridge too high or neck and fingerboard are at incorrect angle to instrument*

B. Bows

Problem	Possible Cause/Solution
Screw turns but frog does not move	Threads in eyelet are stripped—remove and replace
Warped stick	Improperly rehaired or left too long in case fully tightened
Frog does not fit against underside of stick	Eyelet not set at proper depth into frog. Turn eyelet a half- or full-turn into frog
Hair too loose	Left in case fully tightened or exposed to hot and/or humid conditions*
Hair too short	Improperly rehaired*

in a location that provides easiest access. The location is important because some repairs will have to be completed quickly.

1. Repair manuals
2. Instrument cleaner and polish
3. 000 grade steel wool for cleaning strings, fingerboard, and pegs
4. Chin rest wrench for tightening threaded collars
5. Soundpost setters (all instruments) for emergency use only
6. String tuners—above the tailpiece type
7. Assorted bow frog eyelets—sizes are not standardized—for all bows
8. Nylon tail guts (all instruments)
9. Assorted sizes of precut bridges and Roth-DeJacques self-adjusting bridges (all instruments)
10. Peg compound
11. Cleaning liquid for instrument cases
12. Several complete sets of strings for all instruments
13. Rosin cakes and blocks for all instruments
14. Cello and string bass end-pin holders
15. Xylene solution for cleaning caked-on resin

SOME INNOVATIVE PRACTICES IN STRING INSTRUCTION

During the past decades, several personalities and their attendant philosophies and practices have had a profound effect on the overall content and direction of string instruction in America. While some of their individual philosophies may at first appear to be quite different, they are not mutually exclusive; and all practices can be integrated into many aspects of public school string instruction. To a great degree, many of their innovations have application to *all* phases of musical performance—not just strings alone. Some of the most important personalities and practices are summarized here. For individual listings of their publications, see Appendices C and D.

Suzuki and Talent Education

Every now and then there appears on the educational scene a personality whose ideas make a profound and lasting impression on educators throughout the world. Such has been the impact of Shinichi Suzuki and his Talent Education method for teaching strings. As a prospective teacher of string instruments, you should be prepared to discuss the basic principles underlying the Suzuki approach. While your teaching responsibilities may not directly involve you in a Suzuki program, there are many communities throughout the country where Suzuki instruction is available for preschool children. When such instruction is available, it affects the total school music program.

Suzuki's Talent Education method is based on the phi-

losophy that all children possess a splendid capacity for learning if given the opportunity to develop at an early age. Recognizing that children throughout the world have learned to understand and communicate in their mother languages by the age of three, Suzuki reasoned that if they can acquire this sophisticated skill, they can acquire others. In the Suzuki method, children are taught the "language" of music in the same manner as they are taught their "mother tongue"—by listening and through imitation—not note reading.

In an ideal Suzuki "environment," instrumental lessons are not begun until the child has been exposed to a thorough program of listening to high-quality performances on records or tapes. Suzuki recommends that this program should start at birth so that by the time the child is three years old, he or she has acquired a wide listening repertory and is ready to begin instrumental lessons.

One of the unique aspects of this method is parental involvement. Because the child's exposure to language comes primarily from the mother, mothers (or fathers) attend each lesson and actually learn along with the child—taking notes, learning to tune (and/or play) the instrument, and develop the correct concepts of posture and holding the instrument and bow. Also, by supervising daily practice, the parent helps to make music and playing the instrument a family affair.

In the early stages, rote playing is central to Suzuki's approach; all pieces studied are memorized, and music is not used until the students' basic technique is established. As with word reading, note reading is introduced through association. The children watch the notes while they play a piece they have learned from memory. In this way, they are visualizing the symbols that represent the sounds they already know.

One of the many advantages of this approach is the emphasis placed on the *social aspects* of music. In contrast to the students who take a private lesson once a week in a studio and play their instruments with other students only after they have attained a relatively advanced level of accomplishment, students in a Suzuki program play together no matter the level of advancement. Private lessons are encouraged for advancing students, but periodic class participation is required of all students. The more advanced students play with the younger in order to encourage them and demonstrate correct playing habits. In this threefold approach to teaching—teacher, parents, and older students—the prime source for motivation comes from the music and cooperation—not competition.

The great preponderance of Suzuki students in America are studying violin. But the success of the method has been extended to include instruction on cello, piano, and flute.

Samuel Applebaum

The name of Samuel Applebaum is synonymous with the highest standards in string publications and instruction. In his long career, he has produced an immense amount of consistently high-quality materials: well over 250 books, articles, transcriptions, arrangements, etc. In addition to a very busy teaching schedule, he is actively involved in workshops, lectures, and clinics for teachers and students throughout the country, and the production of films and recordings. In his films, Applebaum lectures and demonstrates the basic problems of tone production, shifting, vibrato, bowing studies, etc. Furthermore, the films are a "gold mine" of rote games, procedures, and techniques for teaching strings to children. Throughout his widely used string methods—*String Builder* (five volumes), the *Applebaum String Method: A Conceptual Approach* (three volumes)—there are a number of transcriptions, solos, etudes, and chamber works correlated to the entire series. For the more advanced player, his four-volume series (*The Way They Play*) offers a unique insight into the performance practices of the major string artists.

Kato Havas

The innovative contributions of Kato Havas are the results of her explorations into the origins and causes of the fears and anxieties that tend to become obstacles to playing freedom and expressiveness. Her books reflect the experiences she has acquired from years of teaching her unique approach to performers who have come to her London studio from many points of the globe.

In her books and workshops, she asserts that anxiety, tension, stage fright, etc., are all mental and physical in origin, stemming from our very stressful physical approach to the instrument. An essential aspect of her philosophy is the elimination of tension-producing words (press, strong, hard, forceful, etc.) and the substitution of terms that establish a free and relaxed state: beautiful, giving, lovely, etc. Her "New Approach" is not a static technique that is learned within a single exposure, but an ongoing process wherein the performer seeks out those physical balances and comfort-producing conditions where musical relaxation and expressiveness become an integrated concept.

Though Miss Havas deals with the subjects of tension, fundamental balances, and freedom in performance through the medium of the violin, there are many considerations within her philosophy that are applicable to all instruments.

Paul Rolland

Paul Rolland was quite certainly one of those rare teachers who possessed great experience coupled with the ability for practical application. His career was distinguished not only for his many valuable contributions through his association with the Music Educators National Conference and the American String Teachers Association, as well as his lectures and workshops, but also for his publication of one of the major works in string pedagogy: *The Teaching of Action in Strings.*

This work, written in collaboration with Marla Mutschler, represents the results of five years of research accomplished by the University of Illinois String Research Project, which Mr. Rolland directed. Central to the project's research was the hypothesis that "movement training, designed to free the student from excessive tensions, can be introduced within an organized plan of string instruction, and that such a plan, in the long run, will result in faster learning and better performance in all facets of instruction."

This research culminated in the publication of the book (*The Teaching of Action in Strings*), a series of fourteen films illustrating the seventeen chapters of the book, twenty-two classroom Wall Charts photographically summerizing the principles and exercises in the project, and a Student Book containing the twenty-two Wall Chart photographs and twelve additional pages of Rhythmic Studies for sight reading and bowing exercises. The book, which is profusely illustrated with photographs, diagrams, and musical examples, is also a detailed manual for the film series.

In its totality, *The Teaching of Actions in Strings* is a highly organized course of study that takes the students from their very first lesson through holding the instrument and bow, basic bowing, shifting, and vibrato. While the materials are directed toward training on the violin and viola, there is a universality about the pedagogical devices, motivation techniques, action studies, visual aids, etc., that Mr. Rolland has set forth in his work—concepts that are beneficial to any serious musician.

Appendix A

MINIMUM STANDARDS FOR STRINGED INSTRUMENTS IN THE SCHOOLS

THE String Instruction Committee of the Music Educators National Conference, in cooperation with committee representation from the Music Teachers National Association, the National Association of Schools of Music and the American String Teachers Association, believe that by encouraging the purchase of string instruments and string instrument supplies, which at least meet with the following minimum standards, string instruction and the development of orchestras in the schools can be materially advanced.

Because the "playability" of string instruments depends so much upon proper construction, correct adjustment and alignment, it is hoped these "Minimum Standards for Stringed Instruments in the Schools" will be followed by consumers and teachers and met with by merchants, irrespective of the price bracket in which the instruments happen to fall.

MEASUREMENTS AND TERMINOLOGY OF SIZES

Note: Measurements are given with a "plus or minus (+ or −) sign because instruments of different well-established makers (or even those of the same maker) will vary slightly. It is not the wish of the committee to rule out the many fine instruments that will vary somewhat from the accepted "standards."

A. INSTRUMENT MEASUREMENTS

VIOLIN

Standard (full)	(4/4) body length 14″ + or −	(35.56 cm. + or −)
Intermediate	(3/4) body length 13¼″ + or −	(33.65 cm. + or −)
Junior	(1/2) body length 12-7/16″ + or −	(31.52 cm. + or −)

VIOLA

Standard (full)	(4/4) (large) body length 16½″ and up	(41.9 cm. and up)
	(4/4) body length 15¾″ to 16½″	(40.9 cm. to 41.9)
	(4/4) (small) body length 15″ to 15¾″	(38.1 cm. to 40.9)
Intermediate	body length 14″ + or −	(35.56 cm. + or −)
Junior	body length 13¼″ + or −	(33.65 cm. + or −)

CELLO

Standard (full)	(4/4) body length 29⅝″ + or −	(75.3 cm. + or −)
Intermediate	(3/4) body length 27-5/16″ + or −	(69.4 cm. + or −)
Junior	(1/2) body length 25½″ + or −	(64.77 cm. + or −)

BASS

Standard	(3/4) body length 43¼″ to 44½″ + or −	(109.85 cm. to 113 + or −)
String length from fingerboard nut to bridge	41½″ to 43½″ + or −	(105.4 cm. to 109.85 + or −)
Intermediate	(1/2) body length 41¼″ + or −	(104.8 cm. + or −)
String length from fingerboard nut to bridge	38¾″ + or −	(98.45 cm. + or −)
Junior	(3/8) body length 36⅝″ + or −	(93. cm. + or −)
String length from fingerboard nut to bridge	35″ + or −	(88.9 cm. + or −)

Reprinted with permission from *The String Instruction Program in Music Education.* Copyright © 1957 by the Music Educators National Conference, Reston, Virginia.

B. BOW LENGTH (from tip to end of screw button)

Note: Bows for use with a particular instrument should be the same proportionate size as the instrument, as follows:

Violin (4/4)	29¼"	+ or −	(74.3 cm. + or −)
(3/4)	27"	+ or −	(68.6 cm. + or −)
(1/2)	24-9/16"	+ or −	(62.4 cm. + or −)
Viola Standard	29⅝"	+ or −	(75.2 cm. + or −)
Intermediate	29-3/16"	+ or −	(74.1 cm. + or −)
Junior	27¼"	+ or −	(69.2 cm. + or −)
Cello Standard	28⅛"	+ or −	(71.4 cm. + or −)
Hair length	23¾"	+ or −	(60.3 cm. + or −)
Intermediate	26-7/16"	+ or −	(67.1 cm. + or −)
Hair length	22-1/6"	+ or −	(56.2 cm. + or −)
Junior	24½"	+ or −	(61.6 cm. + or −)
Hair length	20⅜"	+ or −	(51.8 cm. + or −)
***Bass** French Model	28-1/16"	+ or −	(71.5 cm. + or −)
Hair length	21-9/16"	+ or −	(57 cm. + or −)
German (Butler) Model	30⅜"	+ or −	(77.2 cm. + or −)
Hair length	22-1/16"	+ or −	(56 cm. + or −)

MATERIALS AND CONSTRUCTION

A. INSTRUMENTS

1. Back, sides, scroll and top. Wood preferably seasoned seven years before use for instrument construction.
   a. Back sides and scroll—hard maple preferred. (carved).
   b. Top—spruce preferred (carved).
   c. Plywood approved for cellos and basses, thickness to be approved by committee.

2. Construction
   a. All joints glued tightly and reinforced with four full corner blocks and solid upper and lower blocks, full lining inside of top and back. Inlaid purfling preferred.
   b. All edges glued securely.
   c. All cracks, if any, properly repaired (reinforced and glued).
   d. Inlaid purfling strongly preferred over painted purfling.
   e. Bass bar should be of harder spruce than wood used for top itself. Bass bar must be glued in and not carved out from top wood.

3. Trimmings
   a. Pegs—ebony, rosewood, boxwood or cocobola.
   b. Fingerboard:
      (1) First choice—ebony.
      (2) Second choice—rosewood treated to resist absorption (bass and cello only).
   c. Nut and saddle—ebony preferred.
   d. Tailpiece (copper wire loop accepted for elementary school instruments):
      (1) First choice—ebony.
      (2) Second choice—boxwood.
      (3) Third choice—rosewood (cello and bass only).
   e. Cello and Bass end pin:
      (1) Sturdy, metal adjustable, extra long.
      (2) Set screw, extra large "thumb — first finger" grip area.

4. Varnish
   a. Type—good quality of soft texture (oil type varnish preferred; thick hard glossy finish discouraged).
   b. The neck should not be coated with any finish which will prevent the hand from sliding smoothly.
   Recommended process: Wood surfaced with 00 sandpaper and 00 steel wool. Wood wiped with water-moistened cloth to cause loose fibers to "burr," then again rubbed with 00 steel wool; surfaced again with 00 steel wool and, after a second application of linseed oil, polished with a chamois or wool cloth. (Other processes producing this result acceptable.)

5. Attachments
   a. Chinrest—ebony, boxwood or plastic, suitable size, without sharp edges. Player to have choice to suit his own needs.
   b. Strings—should be good quality fresh strings, properly matched.
   Note: The following are recommended for the majority of instruments in most school situations. Climatic conditions and differences in instruments may suggest some deviation.
   (1) Gauges for gut strings (medium):
   Violin - E steel, with adjuster. (See Item 4 "Tuners" below.)
   single strand .010 (.25 mm.) aluminum wound on steel
   .011 (.27 mm.)
   A .029 (.73 mm.) gut
   D .034 (.85 mm.) aluminum on gut
   G .032 (.80 mm.) silver on gut
   Viola - A .029 (.73 mm) gut
   D .035 (.87 mm.) gut or aluminum on gut
   G .033 (.82 mm.) silver on gut
   C .045 (.112 mm.) silver on gut
   Cello - A .044 (1.1 mm.) gut(metal smaller)
   D .051 (1.126 mm.) gut (metal smaller)
   .056 (1.35 mm.) aluminum on gut
   G .054 (1.36 mm.) silverplated wire on gut
   .053 (1.4 mm.) silver on gut
   C .074 (1.75 mm.) silverplated wire on gut or silver on gut
   Bass - G .088 (2.20 mm.) gut
   D .114 (2.85 mm.) gut
   A .110 (2.75 mm.) copper or silver (or plated copper) on gut
   E .138 (3.45 mm.) copper or silver (or plated copper) on gut
   Note: Standardization of large gear box in bass is hoped for.
   (2) Metal strings are supplied by manufacturer in balanced sets.

(3) For general school use, metal strings with tuners (see Item 4 "Tuners" below) approved as follows:

Violin - E single strand .010 (.25 mm.)
             E aluminum wound on steel .011 (.27 mm.)
             A steel core with chromium or aluminum winding over silk or plastic underlay .017 (.43 mm.)
Viola - A (same as Violin A) .017 (.43 mm.)
      D (same as Violin A) .024 (.60 mm.)
Cello - A (same as Violin A) .025 (.625 mm.)
      D (same as Violin A) .036 (.90 mm.)

(4) Tuners (adjusters):

Violin-Viola — type which will not tilt tailpiece or mar top of instrument.
Cello — extra sturdy.

B. BOWS

1. Bow stick.
   a. First choice — Pernambuco, seasoned at least 10 years.
   b. Second choice — metal (aluminum).
   c. Third choice — brazilwood, seasoned at least 10 years.
2. Frogs and tip.
   a. Ebony frog preferred.
   b. Ivory tip preferred; plastic tip acceptable (metal tip acceptable on bass bows.)
   Note: Importers and dealers are urged to standardize eyelet threads on all bows.
3. The bow grip.
   Sterling silver wire with thumb leather at lower end and leather ring at upper end preferred. The leather at both ends should be securely glued or shellacked to stick, and wire should be held together by two runs of solder or other appropriate adhesive. In wrapped bow grips, the winding should not be loose. Thumb leather should be of proper length and thickness at upper end.

C. CASES

1. Type — shaped or oblong type. Hard shell plywood with Keratol, leather or other durable covering preferred. Cases must fit the instrument as well as being of proportionate body area. Special attention should be given to viola cases since there are varied sizes within the 4/4 or standard group.
2. Interior.
   a. Lining soft and attractive (plush material preferred).
   b. Bottom and sides well padded.
   c. At least one accessory pocket and two bow holders.
   d. Zipper instrument cover highly desirable.
3. Zipper cover for case desirable, especially in colder climate.
4. Cello and Bass bags—zipper openings preferred. (Cloth or leather between zipper and bouts.)

ADJUSTMENT

A. PEGS

1. Must be properly fitted to give snug fit at both sides of peg box.
2. Must be lubricated with fresh yellow laundry soap, commercial peg soap, or ordinary chalk.

B. FINGERBOARD

1. Must be straight but slightly concave.
2. Must have medium curvature.

C. NUT

1. Height must be that to give small clearance below strings.
2. Over-all spacing of nut (full or standard size) center of string to string:

Violin	E to G 5/8"	(15.6 mm.)
Viola	A to C 11/16"	(16.9 mm.)
Cello	A to C 7/8"	(21.5 mm.)
Bass	G to E 1-3/16"	(29.6 mm.)

D. BRIDGE

1. Curvature.
   a. Same as the curvature of the fingerboard, but slightly higher on the G string side (E string side for bass).
   b. Material — hard maple preferred.
2. Grooves.
   a. Should be made just deep enough to hold the strings in place.
   b. Should be half round in shape and just large enough to accept the string which it is to accommodate.
   c. Ebony or equivalent inlay desirable under metal strings.
3. Height.
   a. Should be high enough to give the following clearance between strings and end of fingerboard (standard or full-sized instruments; smaller instruments slightly less):

Violin	- E 1/8"	(3.12 mm.)
Violin	- G 3/16"	(4.6 mm.)
Viola	- A 3/16"	(4.6 mm.)
Viola	- C 4/16"	(6.25 mm.)
Cello	- A 1/4"	(6.25 mm.)
Cello	- C 5/16"	(6.80 mm.)
Bass	- G 7/16"	(10.9 mm.)
Bass	- E 11/16"	(17.17 mm).

4. Feet must be shaped to fit the instrument top, bridge tilted backward to form right angle between back side of bridge and top of instrument.
5. Unfitted bridge must be cut to medium thickness and tapered to the top thickness as listed below:

Violin	- 1/16"	(1.55 mm.)
Viola	- 1/16"	(1.55 mm.)
Cello	- 3/32"	(2.32 mm.)
Bass	- 3/16"	(4.67 mm.)

6. Proper string spacing at bridge (center of string to center of string), full size (smaller instruments slightly less):

Violin	- 7/16"	(10.9 mm.)
Viola	- 1/2"	(12.5 mm.)
Cello	- 5/8"	(15.6 mm.)
Bass	- 1-1/8"	(28.1 mm.)

7. Bridge should center on the inner F hole notches.

E. TAILPIECE

1. Gut should be just long enough so that the end of the tailpiece is even with the center of the saddle.
2. Saddle should be high enough so that the tailpiece and ends of tailpiece gut are well in the clear over the top plate. Violin, at least 1/16" proportionately more for other instruments.

F. SOUND POST

1. Location immediately behind the right foot (1st string side) of the bridge. The distance between the back of the bridge and the front of the sound post should be approximately one-half

the thickness of the post (a little more for some instruments).

2. Size:
   Violin - 1/4" (6.1 mm.) diameter
   Viola - 1/4" (6.1 mm.) diameter
   Cello - 7/16" (10.9 mm.) diameter
   Bass - 11/16" (17.1 mm.) diameter

3. Fitting — must fit snugly (but never glued), ends beveled to fit flush with top and back.

G. BOW

1. When the frog is in full forward position, the hair should be relaxed (not loose) and the opposite test should also apply in tightening the bow screw.

2. The hair should be "sighted down" to make sure there are no crossed hairs.

3. The stick (tightened 1½ or 2 rounds for playing) should be "sighted down" to see that it is straight.

4. The frog should seat firmly on the bow, not rock from side to side.

5. The bow screw should work smoothly.

6. The bow grip should be properly attached. (See Item 3 under "Bow Materials").

MISCELLANEOUS

(Direction sheet for Care of Instruments)

A. Keep bow and instrument in case when not in use.
B. Keep bow hair always under slight tension. To use, tighten bow screw only about two (+ or −) rounds.
C. Leave strings always tuned up to pitch.
D. Wipe rosin dust from instrument top and bow stick after playing.
E. Never leave an instrument near a radiator or in a cold room.
F. Do not allow anyone except your teacher to handle your instrument.
G. Have your teacher check frequently for cracks, bridge adjustment, buzzes, etc.
H. Keep case latched (but not locked with the key) when instrument is not in use.
   (Excellent literature on the care of the instrument has been published by leading stringed instrument dealers.)

Appendix B

COMMON ORCHESTRAL TERMS AND NAMES FOR INSTRUMENTS

TERMS

English	Italian	French	German
bow	arco	archet	Bogen
string	corda	corde	Saite
at the point	punta d'arco	(de la) pointe	Spitze
at the frog	al tallone	du talon	am Frosch
at or on the fingerboard	sul tasto (or sulla tastiera)	sur le touche	am Giffbrett
at or near the bridge	sul ponticello	sur le chevalet	am Steg
with the wood of the bow	collegno	avec le bois	mit Holz (or collegno)
mutes or muted	con sordino(i)	sourdine(s)	mit Dämpfer(n)
remove mutes	via sordino	enlevez les sourdines	Dämpfer weg
witout mutes	senza sordino	sans sourdines	ohne Dämpfer
in unison	unisono (unis.)	unis	zusammen (or einfach)
divided	divisi (div.)	divisé (div.)	geteilt (get.)
divided in three parts	div. a 3	div. à 3	dreifach
divided in four parts	div. a 4	div. à 4	vierfach

INSTRUMENTS

English	Italian	French	German
Violin	Violino	Violon	Violine (or Geige)
Viola	Viola	Alto	Bratsche
Violoncello (or Cello)	Violoncello	Violoncelle	Violoncell
Double Bass	Contrabasso	Contre Basse	Kontrabass

Appendix C

SELECTED INSTRUCTIONAL MATERIAL

1. CLASS METHODS

Applebaum, *String Builder* (Belwin)
Bornoff, *Finger Patterns* (Carl Fischer)
Herfurth, *A Tune A Day* (3 Bks.) (Boston Music)
Isaac, *String Class Method* (2 Bks.) (Cole)
Keller-Taylor, *Easy Steps to the Orchestra* (2 Bks.) (Mills)
Muller-Rusch, *Muller-Rusch String Method* (Kjos)
Waller, *String Class Method* (Kjos)
Wisniewski-Higgins, *Learning Unlimited String Program* (Leonard)

2. INDIVIDUAL INSTRUMENTS

VIOLIN

A. Methods, Etudes and Studies

1. Foundation level

Applebaum, *Building Technique with Beautiful Music* (Belwin)
Hirmaly, *Scale Studies* (G. Schirmer)
Matesky-Womack, *The Well-Tempered String Player* (Alfred Music)
Rolland, *Prelude to String Playing* (Boosey & Hawkes)
Wohlfahrt-Aiquoni, *Foundation Studies* (Carl Fischer)

2. Intermediate level

Applebaum, *Orchestral Bowing Etudes* (Belwin)
Dont, *20 Progressive Exercises, Op. 38* (G. Schirmer)
Kayser, *36 Studies, Op. 20* (Nos. 1–12) (G. Schirmer)
Suzuki, *Quint Etudes* (Zen–On Music)
Trott, *Melodious Double-Stops* (Bk. 1) (G. Schirmer)

3. Moderately advanced level

Dont, *24 Exercises, Op. 37* (Carl Fischer)
Kayser, *36 Studies, Op. 20* (Nos. 27–36) (G. Schirmer)
Kreutzer, *42 Studies* (G. Schirmer)
Mazas, *Etudes Special, Op. 36* (Bk. 1) (International Music)
Sevcik, *School of Technique, Op. 1* (Bk. 3) (Carl Fischer)

B. Solos and Collections

1. Foundation level

Dancla, *12 Easy Fantasies, Op. 86* (Carl Fischer)
Herfurth, *Classical Album* (Boston Music)
Perlman, *Violinist's First Solo Album* (Carl Fischer)
Roland-Fletcher, *First Perpetual Motion* (Belwin)
Suzuki, *Suzuki Violin School* (Bks. 1–3) (Zen–On Music)

2. Intermediate Level

Dancla, *Six Airs Varies, Op. 89* (Carl Fischer)
Fiocco, *Allegro* (B. Schott's)
Moffat, *Old Masters for Young Players* (B. Schott's)
Perlman, *Violinist Contest Album* (Carl Fischer)
Suzuki, *Suzuki Violin School* (Bks. 4 & 5) (Zen–On Music)

3. Moderately advanced level

Bach, *Concerto No. 1 in A Minor* (C. F. Peters)
Corelli, *12 Sonatas, Op. 5* (B. Schott's)
Gingold, *Solos for the Violin Player* (G. Schirmer)
Handel, *Six Sonatas* (B. Schott's)
Kreisler, *Liebeslied* (Charles Foley)

VIOLA

A. Methods, Etudes, and Studies

1. Foundation level

Berger, *Basic Viola Technique* (Lee)
Carse, *Viola School* (Augener)
Kreuz, *Selected Studies for the Viola* (Augener)
Lifschey, *Scale and Arpeggio Studies* (G. Schirmer)
Wohlfahrt, *Foundation Studies* (Carl Fischer)

2. Intermediate level

Fischer, *Selected Studies and Etudes* (Belwin)
Kayser, *36 Studies, Op. 43* (International)
Lifschey, *Scale and Arpeggio Studies* (G. Schirmer)

Sevcik-Lifschey, *Selected Studies from Op. 1 and 2* (G. Schirmer)

Whistler, *Introducing the Positions* (Rubank)

3. Moderately advanced studies

Bruni, *Twenty-Five Studies* (Carl Fischer)
Hoffmeister, *12 Studies* (Peters)
Mazas, *Special Etudes, Op. 36* (International)
Primrose, *The Art of Practice of Scale Playing on the Viola* (Belwin)
Vieland, *Orchestral Excerpts* (International)

B. Solos and Collections

1. Foundation level

Bach-Johnstone, *Three Pieces* (Belwin)
Forbes, *A First Year Classical Album* (Oxford)
Hauser, *Berceuse* (Carl Fischer)
Lovell, *44 Easy Tunes* (Oxford)
Murry-Tate, *Tunes Old and New* (Oxford)

2. Intermediate level

Bohm, *Perpetual Motion No. 6 from Third Suite* (Carl Fischer)
Dvořák, *Humoresque, Op. 101, No. 7* (Carl Fischer)
Forbes, *Second Year Classical Album* (Oxford)
Mozart-Elkan, *Sonatina in C Major* (Elkan-Vogel)
Sietz-Lifschey, *Student Concerto No. 2* (Associated)

3. Moderately advanced level

Doktor, *Solos for the Viola Player* (G. Schirmer)
Flackton, *Sonata in G Major* (Schott)
Klengel, *Album of Classical Pieces* (International)
Telemann, *Concerto in G Major* (International)
Telemann-Rood, *Twelve Fantasias for Solo Viola* (McGinnis-Marks)

CELLO

A. Methods, Studies, and Etudes

1. Foundation level

Dotzauer, *Cello Method* (Carl Fischer)
Popper, *15 Easy Studies* (International)
Potter, *Art of Cello Playing* (Summy-Birchard)
Sato-Suzuki, *Sato Cello Method* (Summy-Birchard)
Werner, *Practical Method* (Carl Fischer)

2. Intermediate level.

Epperson, *A Manual of Essential Technique* (Fox)
Klengel, *Daily Exercises* (Breitkopf-Hartel)
Marcelli, *Cello Method* (Carl Fischer)

Matz-Aronson, *The Complete Cellist* (Broude)
Schroeder, *170 Foundation Studies* (Carl Fischer)

3. Moderately advanced level

Duport, *21 Etudes* (G. Schirmer)
Franchomme, *12 Etudes, Op. 35* (International)
Gruetzmacher, *Daily Exercises, Op. 67* (G. Schirmer)
Klengel, *Technical Studies* (Associated)
Kreutzer-Silva, *42 Studies* Peters)

B. Solos and Collections

1. Foundation level

Holleander, *Six Easy Pieces* (Boston)
Krane, *Classical and Folk Melodies* (Presser)
Moffat, *Old Masters for Young Cellists* (Schott)
Otis, *First Book of Study Pieces* (Boston)
Popjoy, *The Singing Cello* (Belwin)

2. Intermediate level

Deri, *Cello Music of French Masters* (G. Schirmer)
Herfurth, *Classical Album of Early Graded Pieces* (Boston)
Hindemith, *Three Easy Pieces* (Schott)
Schroeder, *Violoncello Classics* (Boston)
Squire, *Danse Rustique, Op. 20, No. 5* (Carl Fischer)

3. Moderately advanced level

Bartók, *Roumanian Folk Dances* (Breitkopf-Härtel)
Breval, *Sonata in C Major* (Associated)
Marcello, *Sonatas in C and G Major* (International)
Mendelssohn, *Student Concerto in D Major* (Carl Fischer)
Romberg, *Sonata in B Flat Major, Op. 43, No. 1* (International)

STRING BASS

A. Methods, Studies, and Etudes

1. Foundation level

Findeisen, *Complete Method for the Double Bass* (Presser)
Nanny, *Complete Method for the Double Bass* (Leeds)
Rolland-Krolick, *Prelude to String Playing* (Breitkopf-Härtel)
Simandl, *New Method for Double Bass* (Carl Fischer)
Zimmermann, *Elementary Double Bass Method* (G. Schirmer)

2. Intermediate level

Bille, *New School for the Double Bass* (Ricordi)
Dragonetti, *Five Studies* (Carish)
Lee, *Studies, Op. 31* (International)
Simandl, *30 Etudes* (Carl Fischer)
Storch-Hrabe, *57 Etudes* (International)

3. Moderately advanced level

Lee, *12 Studies* (International)
Ruhm, *Progressive Etudes for the Double Bass* (Doblinger)
Schawabe, *Scale Studies* (International)
Slama, *66 Studies* (Carl Fischer)
Zimmermann, *A Contemporary Concept of Bowing Techniques* (Belwin)

B. Solos and Collections

1. Foundation level

Baklanova, *Ten Easy Pieces* (Leeds)
Chopin-Zimmermann, *Maiden's Wish* (Carl Fischer)
Dalley, *Songs for Strings* (Kjos)
Lesinsky, *Thirty-Four String Bass Solos* (Belwin)
Whistler, *Solos for Strings* (Rubank)

2. Intermediate level

Anderson, *Sonatina* (Carl Fischer)
Bach-Zimmermann, *Gavotte and Minuet* (Carl Fischer)
Martin, *Pompola* (Carl Fischer)
Pergolese, *Tre Giorni* (Carl Fischer)
Ratez, *Six Characteristic Pieces* (Associated)

3. Moderately advanced level

Bottesini, *Reverie* (Carl Fischer)
Capuzzi, *Concerto* (Breitkopf-Härtel)
Galliard, *Sonata in F Major* (International)
Simandl, *Concert Study, Sarabande, and Gavotte* (International)
Zimmermann, *Solos for the Double Bass Player* (G. Schirmer)

For additional sources, see Appendix D, 1.h., "Graded Lists of Solo and Ensemble Literature."

Appendix D
SOURCE MATERIALS

1. SUGGESTED READINGS

a. General Interest

Applebaum, Samuel and Sada, *The Way They Play* (Books I–IV). Neptune City, N.J.: Paganiniana Publications, 1973–1976.

——, *With the Artists*. Rockville Centre, L.I.: Belwin, 1958.

Farga, Franz, *Violins and Violinists*. London: The Camelot Press, 1955.

The Music Industry Council Guide for Music Educators. Reston, Va.: MENC,* 1976.

Reuter, Fritz, *How to Buy a Violin*. Chicago, Il.: Fritz Reuter and Sons, 1972.

Ritsema, Robert Allen, *A History of the American String Teachers Association: The First Twenty-Five Years*. Bryn Mawr, Pa.: Theodore Presser Company for ASTA, 1973.

Tertis, Lionel, *My Viola and I: A Complete Autobiography*. London: Elek Books, 1974.

Wassell, Albert W., and Charles H. Wertman, *Bibliography for String Teachers*. Rev. ed. Reston, Va.: MENC, 1964.

b. Teaching the Strings

Barret, Henry, *The Viola: Complete Guide for Teachers and Students*. University, Al.: University of Alabama Press, 1972.

Berman, Joel, and Barbara Seagrave, *Dictionary of Bowing Terms*. Bryn Mawr, Pa.: Theodore Presser Company for ASTA, n.d.

Celentano, John P., "The Importance of Chamber Music for the String Student," *American String Teacher*, XXII, 4 (Autumn 1973), p. 12.

Colwell, Richard, J., *The Teaching of Instrumental Music*. New York: Appleton-Century-Crofts, Educational Division, Meredith Corporation, 1969.

Cook, Clifford A., *Essays of a String Teacher: Come Let Us Rosin Together*. Jericho, N.Y.: Exposition Press, Inc., 1973.

*Hereafter, MENC.

——, *String Teaching and Some Related Topics*. Bryn Mawr, Pa.: Theodore Presser Company for ASTA, 1957.

Dolejsi, Robert, *Modern Viola Technique*. Chicago, Il.: University of Chicago Press, 1939.

Durflinger, Louis, "Starting the String Class," *Orchestra News*, XI, 4 (September 1972), p. 11.

Epperson, Gordon, *A Manual of Essential Cello Techniques*. New York, N.Y.: Sam Fox, 1974.

Flesch, Carl, *The Art of Violin Playing, Volumes I and II*. New York, N.Y.: Carl Fischer, 1924, 1930.

Galamian, Ivan, *Principles of Violin Playing and Teaching*. Englewood Cliffs, N.J.: Prentice-Hall, 1962.

Green, Elizabeth, *Orchestral Bowings and Routines*. Ann Arbor, Mich.: Ann Arbor Publishers, 1957.

——, *Teaching Stringed Instruments in Classes*. Englewood Cliffs, N.J.: Prentice-Hall, 1966.

Havas, Kato, *A New Approach to Violin Playing*. London: Bosworth, 1961.

Horsfall, Jean, *Teaching the Cello to Groups*. London: Oxford University Press, 1974.

Kievman, Louis, *Practicing the Viola Mentally-Physically*. Pacific Palisades, Ca.: Kelton Publications, n.d.

Krolick, Edward, *Basic Principles of Double-Bass Playing*. Reston, Va.: MENC, 1959.

Kuhn, Wolfgang, *Principles of String Class Teaching*. Rockville Centre, N.Y.: Belwin, 1957.

Lamb, Norman, *A Guide to Teaching Strings*. Dubuque, Iowa: Wm. C. Brown, 1971.

Lorrin, Mark, *Dictionary of Bowing and Tonal Techniques for Strings*. Denver, Co.: Charles Hansen Educational Music and Books, 1968.

Mantel, Gerhard, *Cello Technique: Principles and Forms of Movement*. Trans. Barbara Haimberger Thiem. Bloomington: Indiana University Press, 1975.

Mason, James A., "Individualizing Instruction for the String Class," *Orchestra News*, XII, No. 3 (June 1973), p. 7.

Matz, Rudolf, *The Complete Cellist (Books I and II)*. Trans. Lev Aronson. New York, N.Y.: Alexander Broude, 1974.

Potter, Louis Alexander, *The Art of Cello Playing: A Complete Textbook Method for Private or Class Instruction*. Evanston, Il.: Summy-Birchard, 1964.

——, *Basic Principles of Cello Playing*. Reston, Va.: MENC, 1957.

Rolland, Paul, *Basic Principles of Violin Playing*. Reston, Va.: MENC, 1959.

Rolland, Paul, and Marla Mutschler, *The Teaching of Action in String Playing*. Urbana, Il.: Illinois String Research Associates, 1974.

Primrose, William, *Technique Is Memory*. New York: Oxford University Press, 1960.

Smith, G. Jean, *Cellist's Guide to the Core Technique*. Bryn Mawr, Pa.: Theodore Presser Company for ASTA, 1974.

The String Instruction Program in Music Education. Reston, Va.: MENC, 1957–59. A series of 10 reports prepared by the MENC String Instruction Committee.

Trzcinski, Louis C., *Planning the School String Program*. New York: Mills Music, 1963.

Turetzky, Burtram, *The Contemporary Contrabass*. Berkeley, Ca.: University of California Press, 1974.

Young, Phyllis, *Playing the String Game: Strategies for Teaching Cello and Strings*. Austin, Tx.: University of Texas Press, 1978.

c. Talent Education and Suzuki

Fayssoux, Frank S., "A Man for All Children," *Orchestra News*, VIII, 3 (May 1969), p. 10.

Garson, Alfred, "Learning with Suzuki: Seven Questions Answered," *Music Educators Journal*, LVI, 6 (February 1970), p. 64.

——, "Suzuki and Physical Movement," *Music Educators Journal*, LX, 4 (December 1973), pp. 34–37.

Goodnow, Billie, "Suzuki's 10 New Vital Points," *Orchestra News*, XII, 2 (March 1973), p. 8.

Hermann, Evelyn, "The Suzuki Philosophy—Fallacies and Facts," *American String Teacher*, XXI, 2 (Spring 1971), p. 41.

Honda, Masaaki, *Suzuki Changed My Life*. Chicago, Il.: Summy-Birchard, 1976.

Kendall, John, "The Resurgent String Program in America," *Perspectives in Music Education: Source Book III*. Reston, Va.: MENC, 1966.

——, *The Suzuki Violin Method in American Education*. Reston, Va.: MENC, 1973.

——, *Talent Education and Suzuki*. Reston, Va.: MENC, 1966.

Lang, Sally, "Suzuki Philosophy: What it is—What it is Not," *Orchestra News*, XI, 4 (September 1972), pp. 8–9.

McDonald, Marjorie, M.D., "A Psychoanalyst Looks at Suzuki," *Orchestra News*, XI, 2 (March 1972), p. 5.

——, "The Suzuki Method, Child Development, and Transitional Tunes," *American String Teacher*, XX, 1, 1970.

Mills, Elisabeth, and Sr. Terese Cecile Murphy, eds., *The Suzuki Concept: An Introduction to a Successful Method for Early Music Education*. Berkeley, Ca.: Diablo Press, 1975.

——, *In the Suzuki Style: A Manual for Raising Musical Consciousness in Children*. Berkeley, Ca.: Diablo Press, 1974.

Shetler, Donald J., "I Wonder if the Suzuki Idea Would Work Here?" *Orchestra News*, VII, 3 (May 1968), p. 9.

Spry, Edward N., "The Suzuki Idea *Does* Work Here!" *Orchestra News*, VII, 4 (September 1968), p. 10.

Starr, William, *The Suzuki Violinist: A Guide for Teachers and Parents*. Knoxville, Tn.: Kingston Ellis Press, 1976.

Zahtilla, Paul, *Suzuki in the String Class*. Evanston, Il.: Summy-Birchard, 1971.

d. Recruitment and Public Relations

Gaines, Joan B., *Approaches to Public Relations for the Music Educator*. Reston, Va.: MENC, 1968.

——, "Building Community Support for the Music Program," *Music Educators Journal*, LVIII, 5 (January 1972), pp. 33–64.

Hobbs, Lois. L., "Reminiscing on Recruiting," *American String Teacher*, XXV, 2 (Spring 1975), p. 29.

Hoppe, William H., chairman, *Recruiting Strings in the Schools*. Reston, Va.: MENC, 1957.

Ladd, Donald, "Do You Need Public Relations?" *Orchestra News*, XIII, 2 (1974), p. 3.

Lorrin, Mark, "Promotional Devices that Work," *Orchestra News*, XI, 2 (March 1972), p. 11.

Muller, J. Frederick, "What Is Your Public-Relations Quotient?" *Orchestra News*, XIII, 2 (1974), p. 3.

Shepard, John W., chairman, *String Teacher and Music Dealer Relations and Problems*. Reston, Va.: MENC, 1957.

e. Jazz, Pop, Rock, and Strings

Baker, David, "How to Use Strings in Jazz," *Orchestra News*, XIV, 3 (September 1974), p. 11.

——, "The String Approach to Jazz—Part I," *Orchestra News*, IX, 2 (March 1970), p. 5.

——, "The String Approach to Jazz—Part II," *Orchestra News*, IX, 3 (May 1970), p. 8.

——, "The String Approach to Jazz—Part III," *Orchestra News*, IX, 4 (September 1970), p. 10.

Redmond, Edgar R., "Jazz, Strings and the World of Music," *Orchestra News*, X, 1 (1970) p. 6.

——, "Jazz, Strings and the World of Music—Deserves a Chance," *American String Teacher*, XXI, 3 (Summer 1971), p. 23.

Roberts, John T., "Jazz and Rock in the Curriculum?— Yes!" *Orchestra News*, XI, 2 (March 1972), p. 10.

White, Anderson, "How to Use Strings in Jazz," *Orchestra News*, XIV, 1 (December 1974), p. 11.

Wilson, George H., "Strings in the Jazz Idiom?—Why Not?" *Orchestra News*, XII, 3 (June 1973), p. 6.

Wolfrom, Lyle, "The String Bass in Jazz, Folk, and Rock," *American String Teacher*, XXIV, 2 (Spring 1974), p. 22.

f. History and Physics of Instruments and Bows

Boyden, David, *The History of Violin Playing from its Origins to 1761*. London: Oxford University Press, 1965. The recording enclosed illustrates the sound of a modern violin (with modern bow) compared to an "old" violin (with old-style bow).

Dolmetsch, Natalie, *Viola da Gamba*. New York: Henrichsen Edition, 1968.

Geminiani, Francesco, *The Art of Playing on the Violin (1751)*. Ed. by David Boyden. New York: Oxford University Press, 1968.

Goldsmith, Pamela, "Viotti and the Tourte Bow," *American String Teacher*, XXIII, I (Winter 1973), p. 20.

Hutchens, Carleen M., and Marjorie Bram, "The Bowed Strings—Yesterday, Today, Tomorrow." *Music Educators Journal*, LX, 3 (November 1973), pp. 20–25.

———, "The Physics of Violins," *Scientific American*, November 1962, p. 81.

Jalovec, Karel, *Beautiful Italian Violins*. New York: Tudor Press, 1964.

Kinney, Gordon J., "The Viols and Their Cousins: An Historical Note," *American String Teacher*, XXIII, 2 (Spring 1973), p. 12.

Nelson, Sheila M., *The Violin and Viola*. London: Ernest Benn, 1972.

Panum, Hortense, *The Stringed Instruments of the Middle Ages*. New York: Da Capo Press, 1971.

Retford, William C., *Bows and Bow Makers*. London: The Strad, 1964.

Roda, Jospeh, *Bows for Musical Instruments of the Violin Family*. Chicago: William Lewis, 1959.

Stoeving, Paul, *The Violin: Its Famous Makers and Players*. Westport, Ct.: Greenwood Press, 1970. Originally published in 1928 by Oliver Ditson Company, Boston.

van der Straeten, E., *The History of the Violin, Volumes I and II*. London: Cassell, 1933. Reprinted by Da Capo Press, 1968.

von Wasielewski, Wilhelm Joseph, *The Violincello and Its History*. Trans. Isobella S. E. Stigand. New York: Da Capo Press, 1968.

Wechsberg, Joseph, *The Glory of the Violin*. New York: Viking Press, 1973.

g. Instrumental Repairs

Bearden, Lowell and Douglas, *Emergency String Repair Manual for School Orchestra Directors*. Elon, N.C.: Elon College Press, 1972.

Burgan, Arthur, *Basic String Repairs*. London: Oxford University Press, 1974.

You Fix Them. Cleveland, Ohio: Sherl & Roth, n.d.

Zurfluh, John, ed., "Clampers' Corner—String Repair Column," *American String Teacher*, issues beginning 1972.

h. Graded Lists of Solo and Ensemble Literature

Barrett, Henry, *The Viola: Complete Guide for Teachers and Students*. University, Al.: University of Alabama Press, 1972. Graded Lists (10 levels) for viola, pp. 12–32.

De Runges, Maria, *Cello Syllabus*. Napa, Ca.: Motty's Olde Colony Press, 1972.

Dillon, Jacquelyn, *A Listing of Full Orchestra, String Orchestra, and String Ensemble Materials (Grade I–VI)*. Cleveland, Oh.: Educational Division, Scherl and Roth, n.d.

Fitts, Muriel, *Selected String Orchestra Literature: Easy–Intermediate*. Bryn Mawr, Pa.: Theodore Presser Company for ASTA, 1963.

Grodner, Murray, *Comprehensive Catalogue of Available Literature for the Double Bass*. 3rd ed. Bloomington, Ind.: Lemur Musical Research, 1971.

Gundling, Dorothy, *Music Guide for String Classes*. Napa, Ca.: Motty's Olde Colony Press, 1971.

Krolick, Edward J., "Graded List of Double Bass Solo Music," *Double Bass Handbook*. Urbana, Il.: University of Illinois Press, n.d.

Matesky, Ralph, chairman, *A Compendium of Recommended School Orchestra Literature*. Bryn Mawr, Pa.: Theodore Presser Company for ASTA, 1965.

Oppelt, Robert, *Graded and Annotated List of Music for the Student Violist*. Bryn Mawr, Pa.: Theodore Presser Company for ASTA, 1971.

Potter, Louis Alexander, *The Art of Cello Playing: A Complete Textbook Method for Private or Class Instruction*. Evanston, Il.: Summy-Birchard, 1964. Chapter 36, "Appendix: Cello Repertoire List," pp. 218–224.

Rolland, Paul, chairman, *String Syllabus—Revised 1975*. Bryn Mawr, Pa.: Theodore Presser Company for ASTA, 1975.

Selective Music Lists—1979: Instrumental Solos and Ensembles. Reston, Va.: MENC. 1979.

String Music: Recommended and Graded. New York: Carl Fischer, n.d.

University Interscholastic League Prescribed Music List. Box 8028, University Station, Austin, Tx. 78712.

i. Periodicals

American String Teacher. Bryn Mawr, Pa.: Theodore Presser Company for American String Teachers Association, 19010.

The Instrumentalist. Evanston, Il.: The Instrumentalist Company, 1418 Lake St., 60202.

Music Educators Journal. Reston, Va.: Music Educators National Conference, 1902 Association Drive, 22091.

Music Journal. 370 Lexington Avenue, New York, N.Y. 10017.

The Music Register. Magnolia, Ark.: P.O. Box 94, 71753.

Orchestra News. Cleveland, Oh.: Scherl and Roth, Inc., 1729 Superior St., 44114.

The School Musician. Joliet, Ill.: 4 East Clinton St., P.O. Box 245, 60434.

World of Strings. Philadelphia, Pa.: William Moennig & Sons, Inc., 2039 Locust St., 19103.

The Strad. London: J. H. Lavender & Co., 2 Duncan Terrace, London, N.1.

2. PROFESSIONAL ORGANIZATIONS

ASTA American String Teachers Association

MENC Music Educators National Conference
NSOA National School Orchestra Association
VFG Viola-Forchungsgesellschaft (Viola Research Society)
VSA Violin Society of America

3. STRING INSTRUMENTS AND SUPPLIES

Bein and Fushi, Fine Arts Building, Suite 1014, 410 South Michigan Ave., Chicago, Ill. 60605.

Karnes Music Company, 9800 Milwaukee Avenue, Des Plaines, Ill.

William Lewis & Sons, 7373 N. Cicero Avenue, Lincolnwood, Ill. 60646.

Shar Products Company, P.O. Box 1411, Ann Arbor, Mich. 48106.

Scherl and Roth, Inc., 1729 Superior Avenue, Cleveland, Ohio 44114.

Andrew Schroetter and Company, Inc., 55 Marcus Drive, Melville, N.Y. 11746.

Phillip H. Weinkrantz Musical Supply Company, 3715 Dickanson Avenue, Dallas, Tex. 75219.

4. FILMS AND FILMSTRIPS

Argo Record Company
115 Fulham Road
London S.W.3., England

Artist Films, Inc.
366 Madison Avenue
New York, New York 10016

Stanley Bowmar Co.
12 Cleveland Street
Valhalla, New York 10595

Brandon Films
200 West 57th Street
New York, New York 10019

Brigham Young University
Department of Audio-Visual Communications
Provo, Utah

Encyclopaedia Britannica Films, Inc.
1150 Wilmette Avenue
Wilmette, Illinois 60091

Classroom Film Distributors, Inc.
5620 Hollywood Blvd.
Los Angeles, California 90007

Coronet Instructional Films
Coronet Building
65 East South Water Street
Chicago, Illinois 60601

Film Association of California
11559 Santa Monica Blvd.
Los Angeles, California 90019

Jim Handy Organization
2821 East Grand Blvd.
Detroit, Michigan 48211

Indiana University
Audio-Visual Center
Bloomington, Indiana 47405

Irving Lesser Enterprises
527 Madison Avenue
New York, New York 10019

Scherl and Roth, Inc.
1729 Superior Street
Cleveland, Ohio 44114

Sterling Educational Films
241 East 34th Street
New York, New York 10018

University of Michigan TV
310 Maynard Street
Ann Arbor, Michigan 48108

University of Nebraska
Bureau of Audio-Visual Instruction
Lincoln, Nebraska 68508

INDEX